VOLUME 17

BELL P-39/P-63
AIRACOBRA & KINGCOBRA

BY FREDERICK A. JOHNSEN

PUBLISHERS AND WHOLESALERS

Published by
Specialty Press Publishers and Wholesalers
11481 Kost Dam Road
North Branch, MN 55056
United States of America
(612) 583-3239

Distributed in the UK and Europe by
Airlife Publishing Ltd.
101 Longden Road
Shrewsbury
SY3 9EB
England

ISBN 1-58007-010-8

Material contained in this book is intended for historical and
entertainment value only, and is not to be construed as usable
for aircraft or component restoration, maintenance or use.

Designed by Greg Compton

Printed in the United States of America

TABLE OF CONTENTS

THE BELL P-39/P-63 AIRACOBRA & KINGCOBRA

FOREWORD

The author, Frederick A. Johnsen, has had a unique relationship with the Bell P-39 Airacobra. As a youngster five years old, he became fascinated with the box art illustration on a ninety-eight cent Revell model kit of the Airacobra. He would gaze at it by the hour in the dime store — he couldn't afford to buy it.

Times have changed. Instead of being a wanna-be-owner of a model airplane kit, Fred is one of the very few individuals in the world who is the owner of a real P-39 — one with a combat record at that. It is one of several salvaged from the jungles of New Guinea by warbird collector David Tallichet back when such an operation was still possible.

Fred, who is currently an Air Force historian, is also a noted free-lance writer. He is a former editor of *Western Flyer* (now simply *The Flyer*, a twice-monthly aviation newspaper), and the author of five other books in the WarbirdTech series.

Ever since his wishful days with the model kit, Fred has maintained a special interest in the P-39, and is well-qualified to write about it in a "warts and all" coverage that deals with its technical was well as operational shortcomings and is able to put some of the Airacobra horror stories into proper perspective.

As a first lieutenant in the AAF in 1944, I was Assistant Engineering Officer for the 69th Sub-Depot at McChord Field, Washington, when a production-line maintenance program was established to refurbish war-weary P-39s for service at U.S. Army fighter pilot schools. In addition to being involved with the technical problems of the P-39, I was also the weight-and-balance officer, responsible for maintaining the P-39's critical center-of-gravity location after the removal of guns and armor and the redistribution of other equipment.

I have known Fred since his high school days and am pleased to be able to draw on my own technical experience with the P-39 to be able to enthusiastically endorse his work.

Peter M. Bowers
Seattle, Washington
February, 1998

Peter M. Bowers, then an Engineering Officer with the Air Service Command in India, shown with a Free-French B-17F

WARBIRDTECH
SERIES

PREFACE

Chuck Yeager enjoyed the sleek little P-39 Airacobra. Some other pilots damned it as a tumbling deathtrap. Soviet airmen embraced its low-altitude performance and made a fearsome ground attack weapon of the P-39. Latter-day magazine articles ridiculed its performance in the air-to-air combat arena. And Bell pilot Tex Johnston raced an Airacobra to glory. Somewhere in this wilderness of differing opinions and exploits resides the true nature of this pioneering tricycle-gear warplane.

Close on the heels of the art-deco P-39 Airacobra came the functionally-altered P-63 Kingcobra, with newer laminar-flow airfoil, two-stage mechanical supercharger, and an angular no-nonsense appearance that seemed to telegraph the Kingcobra's ability to rectify any deficiencies attributed to its predecessor, the P-39. Together, the Airacobra and Kingcobra put Bell Aircraft Corporation on the map. Two years after the end of World War Two, it was another Bell product, the frugally streamlined X-1 rocket aircraft, that propelled the world into the age of supersonic flight. It's not surprising that the young aircraft company innovative enough to design the Airacobra around a center-mounted engine and tricycle landing gear was also the free-thinking creator of the world's first supersonic aircraft.

If the P-39 was wanting in performance at altitude, adaptable fliers made the most of its other strengths. While analysis of the Airacobra's capabilities is useful to a point, no amount of second-guessing can change history. The story of the P-39 and, to a lesser extent the P-63, stands as a testimonial to the men and women who built, serviced, and flew the 'Cobras around the world. My interest in the P-39 is more than academic. In 1987 I began research and parts-gathering for a P-39N-5, number 42-19027. The trail has led me to a variety of people and interesting finds over the past decade.

Thanks are due to many who helped expand my P-39 and P-63 research files. They include: Don Alberts, Peter M. Bowers, Clover Park Vocational Technical Institute (and Mike Potter), the Confederate Air Force, Bob Etter, the Experimental Aircraft Association, Wayne Fiamengo, Tom Foote, E.F. Furler, Ben Howser, Larry Jaynes, Sharon Lea Johnsen, Alvin M. "Tex" Johnston, Don Keller (Air Depot), Birch Matthews, Dave Menard (and the U.S. Air Force Museum), Allan Metscher, Bill Miranda, L.M. Myers, Leo Oestreicher, Merle C. Olmsted, Garry Pape, Dennis Parks, Milo Peltzer, Doug Remington, Carl Schuler, Don Thomson, U.S. Air Force Historical Research Agency, and Ray Wagner (and the San Diego Aerospace Museum).

Abbreviations used in some photo credits include AFHRA (Air Force Historical Research Agency), EAA (Experimental Aircraft Association), SDAM (San Diego Aerospace Museum), and USAFM (United States Air Force Museum.

FREDERICK A. JOHNSEN
1998

Head-on view of the unflown XP-39 taken in October 1938 shows early nosewheel configuration that left part of the wheel exposed even when retracted; production Airacobras had fully-enclosed nosewheels that nested in a bump in the cockpit floor. Engine coolant radiator inlet is visible in leading edge of aircraft's left wing. (Bell photo)

P-39 DESIGN & DEVELOPMENT

The young Bell Aircraft Corporation charted a course based on innovation. Its first two original aircraft designs were the unorthodox twin-pusher FM-1 Airacuda fighter and the mid-engine, tricycle-wheeled XP-39 Airacobra. The Airacobra was the Airacuda's antithesis, light and compact. But the Bell team's penchant for innovation was manifest in the XP-39, which used as its basic premise a mid-fuselage location for the Allison V-1710 engine, freeing up the nose for an impressive 37-MM cannon, ammunition stowage, and space for a retractable nosewheel.

Originally devising an aft location for the cockpit, behind the engine and just ahead of the tail, Bell designers discarded this in favor of an automobile-style cabin atop the wing, just ahead of the engine. A two-segment drive shaft, turning at crankcase RPMs, passed beneath the cockpit to a gearbox in the extreme nose. In this way, the drive shaft was below centerline, relying on planetary gears in the gearbox to transfer the power to the propeller. This kept the centerline open for the cannon, which fired through the large spinner.

Adding to the P-39's automobile appearance were two cabin doors that hinged at the front, and even had roll-down safety glass windows. A turbosupercharger gave the XP-39 performance at altitude.

The Allison V-1710-E-series engine adapted for the Airacobra gave rise to the equation of its series letter — *E* — with Extension, as a means of identifying P-39 engines which relied on an extension drive shaft to reach the gearbox in the nose of the aircraft. Though this became a convenient way to remember Airacobra Allisons, writer Pat Plummer, in *Wings* magazine, says the origin is more prosaic: The E-series used in the P-39 simply followed Allison's D-series engines used in the earlier Bell Airacuda.[1]

In theory, the center location for the mass of the Allison V-12 engine should provide good maneuverability. (Later, in combat, the P-39 was found to have a larger turning radius than the Mitsubishi A6M Zero, a fate shared by other American fighters too.) Bell engineers designed a turbosupercharger installation beneath the Allison in the XP-39's fuselage, to aid altitude performance. The turbosupercharger's cooling radiator duct bulged from the left side of the fuselage. Given Army serial number 38-326, the XP-39 was completed in 1938. Disassembled in New York and transported to Wright Field where it was put together for its first flight, the XP-39 took to the air for the first time on 6 April 1939. Retired Navy pilot James Taylor made the first flight. Ballasted (because it lacked armament) and weighing in at barely over 6,200 pounds, the XP-39 proved capable of climbing to 20,000 feet over the verdant Ohio countryside near Wright Field in five minutes. Its

XP-39 on the ramp at Wright Field in February 1939 shows cutouts in original nosewheel doors for protruding tire when retracted. Forked main gear doors gave way to other design iterations. Propeller cuffs were not retained in production P-39s. Large turbosupercharger intercooler duct on the side of the fuselage added to drag; actual turbosupercharger nested in ventral location. (Oliver Phillips collection via Peter M. Bowers)

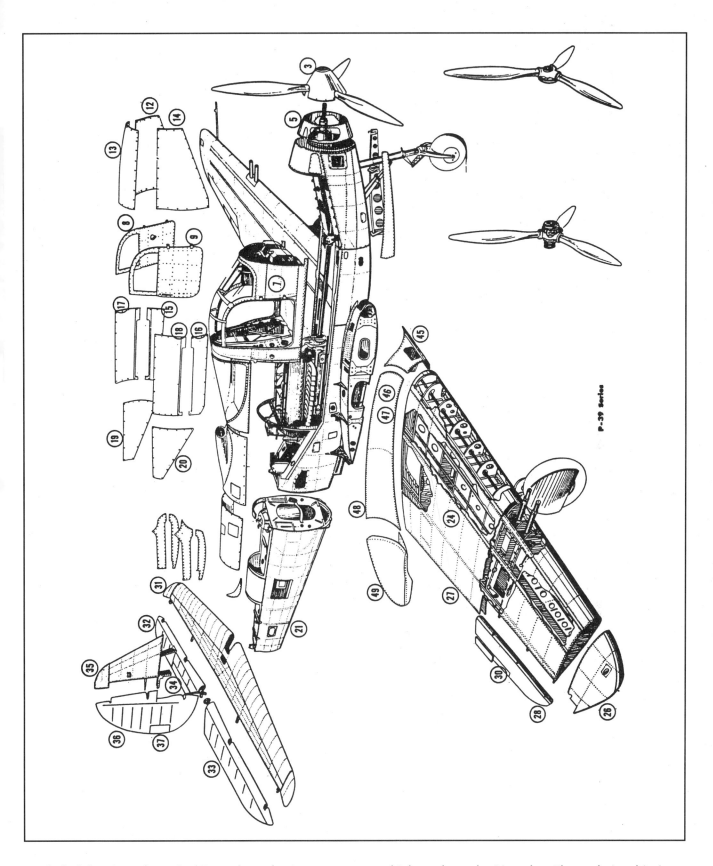

Exploded drawing of a typical P-39 shows basic components which made up the Airacobra. The cockpit cabin (part 7) was built as a unit that attached to the lower beams of the forward fuselage. Drawing makes accommodation for Curtiss Electric and Aeroproducts propellers, both of which were widely used on P-39s. Removable stiffeners (not shown) held cowlings in place.

XP-39 (serial number 38-326) had higher canopy than subsequent Airacobras, and smaller vertical fin, as photographed at Wright Field. (Peter M. Bowers collection)

speeds reached toward 390 miles an hour, although historian Birch Matthews suggests this may have been a calculated speed, and that actual speeds attained may have been lower, giving urgency to Bell's subsequent actions with the aircraft's design. Regardless, it is agreed that the XP-39 did not breach 400 miles an hour.

Disappointed at the inability to crack the 400-mile-per-hour speed range, Bell Aircraft sent the XP-39 to the NACA (National Advisory Committee for Aeronautics) full-

scale wind tunnel in Langley, Virginia, in the summer of 1939, with about 60 hours on the airframe. NACA engineers enjoyed a reputation for solving aerodynamic problems for American aircraft manufacturers. The result of a review of the XP-39 design, and the NACA wind tunnel tests, was to remove the turbosupercharger from the left side of the fuselage, move the carburetor inlet to a dorsal location, lower the height of the cockpit canopy, cut a total of 22 inches from the span of the wings, down to 34 feet, add 13 inches to fuselage length, and replace the original V-1710-17 engine with a Dash-39 variant.[2]

Few decisions in World War Two aircraft development have received as much attention and speculation as the choice to remove the turbosupercharger from the XP-39. Given the proven business acumen of company founder Larry Bell, his enthusiasm for removing the turbosupercharger suggests this was not a half-baked notion. Not only did the fuselage installation of the turbosupercharger degrade XP-39 performance, as proven in NACA wind tunnel tests, the state of the art for turbosuperchargers in the 1939-40 period was less than mature. Unlike the twin-boom Lockheed P-38, where no frantic need to upgrade performance was noted (and possibly because Lockheed had some other contracts to cushion its financial statement), the diminutive XP-39 was dogged by its drag-inducing, and not always reliable, turbosupercharger. To these negatives was added the positive argument that Allison was improving its V-1710 engine continually, and that advances in mechanical supercharging would make up for the loss of the turbine-

As evolved into the XP-39B, the first Airacobra tried teardrop maingear doors and truncated nosewheel doors with a long door attached to the strut. Canopy was lowered to reduce drag. (Bell, via Bowers)

WARBIRD**TECH**
S E R I E S

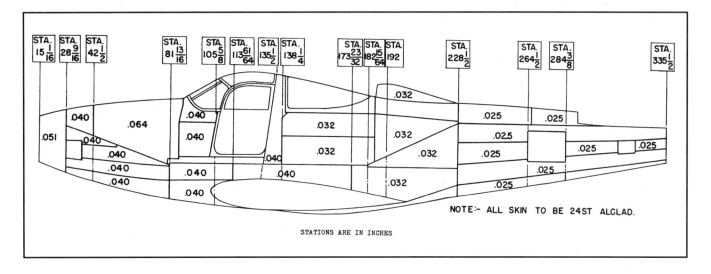

As depicted for the P-400, Airacobra fuselage stations and skin thicknesses are shown in a line drawing from the "Dash-3" Structural Repair manual. (Courtesy Glen Spieth)

wheel turbocharger, if maybe at slightly lower altitudes.

From a pragmatic standpoint, Bell needed to go into production of Airacobras to ensure a positive cash flow, rather than tinker with perfecting a turbosupercharger installation in the Airacobra; some in the Air Force likewise saw the need for many fighters quickly, and blessed the decision to delete the turbosupercharger from the P-39 as an expedient. To be sure, the turbosupercharger ultimately was developed into the reliable device so valuable to P-38s, P-47s, B-17s, B-24s, and B-29s, but it is well to remember the vaunted P-51 Mustang was boosted to altitude by a mechanical supercharger. (As events unfolded, Allison developed a competitive mechanical supercharger too large to fit in a regular P-39, but just in time for the accommodatingly-larger P-63 Kingcobra.)[3]

The revised aircraft, called XP-39B, enjoyed better maneuverability, but top speed was now lessened to 375 miles an hour at only 15,000 feet; plus, it took seven and a half

minutes to even reach 20,000 feet in the XP-39B. Twenty-eight hours into its flight test program, the XP-39B was lost in a crash, joining such other notable prototypes in demise as the XP-38 and Model 299 Flying Fortress. Nonetheless, an Air Corps eager to develop new airplanes liked what they saw of the original XP-39, and ordered 13 service test YP-39s (Bell Model 12) in April 1939 even before the modified XP-39B flew on 25 November of that year.[4]

INTO PRODUCTION

The YP-39s introduced a vertical fin of larger chord, and used V-1710-37 engines. Otherwise, they were close to the specifications of the XP-39B. Weight was climbing to 7,235

Sporting tinted cabin top glazing for a while, the XP-39B shows off its newly-acquired dorsal carburetor scoop, and engine exhausts without the presence of oil cooler ducting, which was relocated to the wing leading edge. Full-length nosewheel doors similar to production models are evident in the photo. (Bell photo)

YP-39 configuration firmed-up many salient Airacobra traits. Broader vertical fin was introduced on the YP-variant. (USAFM)

pounds. Given serials 40-027 through 40-039, the YP-39s were delivered in December 1940 for Air Corps evaluation. Some eventually found their way back to Bell for use as demonstrators developing improvements to the P-39 line. Several were destroyed in accidents into 1943; others were taken out of service.

Paralleling developments and orders for Lockheed's twin-engine P-38 fighter, the YP-39 was succeeded in production by a contract signed back in August 1939 for 80 versions known at Bell Aircraft as the Model 13, and in the Air Corps initially as the P-45, then the P-39C. (Twenty of the batch of 80 were built as C-models before the rest were made as P-39Ds.)

The 20 C-model Airacobras, with a Dash-35 Allison engine, approximated the YP-39s.

Clean-wing P-39C shows basic form of all Airacobras to follow; lack of small dorsal fin fillet and no wing guns are principal visual differences between C- and D-models. (Garry Pape collection)

With the introduction of the P-39D (Bell Model 15), some defining changes occurred: Two .30-caliber guns were removed from the four-gun nose armament and four .30s were placed internally in the wings. The D-model featured a bomb shackle under the wing center section that could alternately carry a jettisonable fuel tank. To make the

Possibly the last P-39C, or the first P-39D (sans dorsal fillet), this un-numbered Airacobra has patches in the leading edge of the wings where .30-caliber machine guns would mount; this aircraft may be the testbed link between P-39Cs and P-39Ds. (USAFM)

WARBIRD**TECH**
S E R I E S

P-39D's internal fuel tanks more combat-suitable, they were self-sealing, at an expense in capacity; they could now tank 120 gallons. A small, but readily visible, change introduced in production on the P-39D was a slight dorsal fin fillet. Orders for P-39D-1 variants were to be delivered to Great Britain's Royal Air Force. A salient difference in Airacobras intended for Britain was the substitution of a 20-MM M1 cannon instead of the hallmark 37-MM weapon. These were followed by P-39D-2BEs, fitted with a Dash-63 engine, and also earmarked for Lend-Lease. The Soviet Union eventually received a substantial portion of the D-1s and D-2s, while others were retained for U.S. squadrons.

The configuration of the P-39D remained essentially unchanged in most fundamental ways through production of subsequent models up to the P-39N; the last production Airacobra, the P-39Q, introduced its own signature in the form of two underslung .50-caliber machine guns in the wings replacing the earlier four internally-carried .30-caliber weapons.

Even with Bell Model 15 P-39D-1s and -2s intended for export, the Bell Model 14 was devised to meet export needs, with the British ordering 675 Model 14s and calling them initially the Caribou — later changing the name to the more aggressive-sounding Airacobra I. The Model 14 also used the 20-MM cannon.

The XP-39E represented efforts by Bell Aircraft to boost Airacobra performance with a new wing of thicker symmetrical section and greater chord, and other modifications. While the squared-off E-model was faster than a production P-39D, it

Early P-39D shows wing guns and dorsal fillet; blisters cover upper nose machine gun ports. Production landing gear door configuration, with angular inboard main flipper doors, is evident. (USAFM)

was also heavier and more sluggish — hardly attributes of a competitive fighter. The first of three P-39Es built crashed in March 1942. Ultimately, the experimental E-models withered in favor of the essentially all-new P-63 Kingcobra, using a laminar flow airfoil. In fact, the legacy of the XP-39E is its use as a testbed for the improved Allison engine with two-stage supercharg-er that did so much to improve performance of the P-63.[5]

P-39Fs were 229 Airacobras essentially the same as D-models, but fitted with three-bladed Aeroproducts propellers instead of the Curtiss-Electric propellers of earlier Airacobras.[6] So close were the F-models to their immediate production predecessor that they were

Crisp P-39D, with censored tail number, has sway braces in place for drop tank. Some D-models used individual exhaust stacks totaling 24 ports, like this example; others used 12 stacks, combining the double-opening of each exhaust on the Allison engine.

Torture test of a P-39D included weighting the wings with bags of heavy shot to replicate positive G-loading. (USAFM)

designated Model 15B at Bell. An additional 25 Airacobras originally intended to round out F-model production at 254 aircraft were completed as P-39Js (see below).[7]

Bell Model 26 was to have been the P-39G, but the 1,800 Airacobras ordered as G-models were actually delivered as P-39Ks, Ls, Ms, and Ns, no G-models being produced. P-39H was not assigned, and the letter "I" was not used by the USAAF to avoid confusion with the digit "1". The next production Airacobra was the P-39J, representing a small number (25) of aircraft from the F-model allocation that were fitted with the V-11710-59 engine and differentiated by the use of the letter "J".

Some Bell Aircraft and USAAF documents do not include the few J-models in tables describing Airacobra characteristics. Serial numbers 41-7053 through 41-7056 and 41-7059 through 41-7079 were assigned to the P-39Js.[8]

Model 26A inherited some of the unbuilt P-39Gs as P-39Ks, with V-1710-63 engines and Aeroproducts propellers. Ordered in the pre-war month of August 1941, 210 K-models were constructed.[9]

The P-39L (Bell Model 26B) was the earliest designation of Airacobra to switch the balloon 19-inch smooth contour (SC) nosewheel tire for a low-profile 6.80x10 tire (although some field switches have been noted in photos of other models of Airacobra.) The P-39L flew behind a Curtiss Electric propeller.[10]

The P-39M (Bell Model 26D) used the 1,200-horsepower V-1710-83 engine and a Curtiss propeller. Top speed of 370 miles an hour at 15,000 feet was a 10 mile-per-hour increase over many previous models.

The P-39N (Bell Models 26C and 26F) settled in to a long production run of 2,095 aircraft. After 166 N-models were built with the 10-foot, 4-inch (sometimes listed as 10-foot, 5-inch) Aeroproducts propeller, a significantly larger 11-foot, 7-inch diameter prop was fitted to the remaining P-39Ns. With four wing fuel cells removed as a weight-savings measure, these N-models attained a top speed of 376 miles an hour at 15,000 feet, and were still pushing 375 miles an hour at 20,000 feet.

The letter "O" was not assigned as an AAF model designator to avoid confusion with the numeral zero; there was no P-39P.

Last, and most numerous, production variant of the Airacobra series

Yarn tufts taped to the wing/fuselage fillet area show airflow patterns in this test photo of a P-39; feathered propeller means prop wash will not affect the airflow pattern for this test. (Bell photo via Peter M. Bowers)

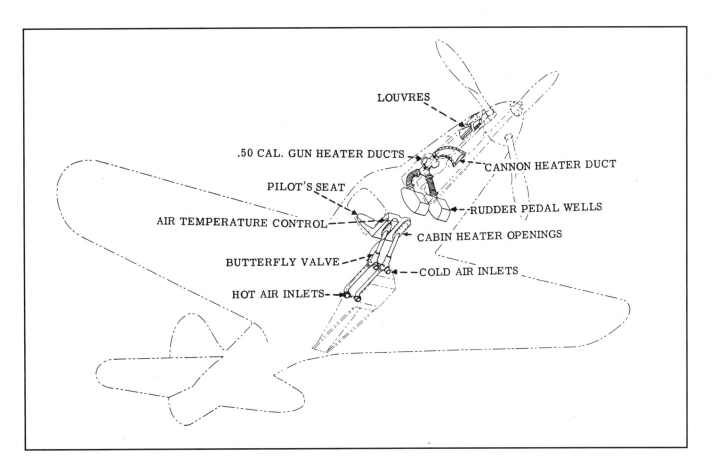

Diagram shows air ducts releasing hot or cold air under the pilot's seat. Rudder pedal wells in front part of cockpit are topped with air ducts to heat the guns in the bay ahead of the cockpit. Airflow pressure was supposed to be higher in the cockpit than in the gun bay, to keep gun gases from bothering the pilot.

was the P-39Q at 4,905 examples built. The easiest recognition feature on P-39Qs was a pair of underwing gondolas, each carrying one .50-caliber machine gun instead of the four internal .30-caliber wing guns of previous Airacobras. However, around production of the P-39Q-20, the underwing gun pods were deleted, reducing the overall firepower. P-39Q-21 and -25 used four-blade Aeroproducts propellers, necessitating some additional sleuthing when identifying close-up nose photos of these variants which can appear much like P-63s. Factory and field modifications varied the number of fuel cells in P-39Qs, and N-models, with corresponding performance changes.[11]

Early P-39D photo is noteworthy for showing downwash to engine exhaust pattern, and silvery Curtiss Electric propeller blades. Many Airacobras, with Curtiss and Aeroproducts propellers, had metallic gray-silver blades instead of painted black blades typically associated with World War Two USAAF aircraft. (USAFM)

One version of the XP-39E tested a two-stage V-1710-47 engine; carburetor air scoop has been moved aft to accommodate the new engine. XP-39E introduced traits that later would surface with the P-63 Kingcobra, including relocated cockpit farther ahead of wing, and nosewheel strut with scissors facing forward, and virtually no aft canting of the forks. (Bell via Bowers)

Overall, the Airacobra's aesthetics survived remarkably intact from the YP-39s to the last Q-models built.

BUILDING THE P-39

Bell Aircraft Corp. president Lawrence D. "Larry" Bell said the P-39 design philosophy hinged on three fundamental assumptions: The fighter must have capable firepower, good pilot visibility, and good landing and ground traits.

The way these goals were addressed was with the singularly unorthodox placement of the engine aft of the pilot.[12]

The same lack of orthodoxy at Bell Aircraft that infused the design of the Airacobra with innovation also led to some creativity on the assembly floor. Bell vice president and general manager O.L. Woodson credited accurate tooling, lofting of even small parts to assure proper

fit, and mechanized assembly lines on a timetable, with giving the company productive construction methods. Writing in *American Machinist* magazine in pre-war 1941, Woodson described the Airacobra's five main subassemblies: 1. forward fuselage; 2. aft fuselage; 3. wings; 4. wing/fuselage carry-through structure; and 5. cockpit cabin. At a time when some aircraft manufacturers still relied on a large amount of hand-fitting of each aircraft, Bell took pride in describing its assembly fixtures used to reproduce each of the five P-39 subassemblies, achieving a repeated accuracy that was said to allow for complete interchangeability of similar subassemblies.[13]

Accuracy in the manufacture of small pieces was said to reduce the need for assembly jigs by 30 percent on production P-39s. Hydraulic presses stamped out many Airacobra parts: Wing and fuselage bulkheads, wing ribs, tail-surface ribs, door panels, instrument panels, control-surface pieces, and floor members. By using two loading tables, crews on either side of the presses could synchronize their use of the machines to maximize output of stampings. Drop hammers formed some parts made from heat-treated alloys or heavier stock, including cowling panels.[14]

Virtually every part of the P-39, including fittings and machined parts, was laid out in full size by the Bell lofting department. This attention to full-size detail allowed for close tolerances and a high degree of interchangeability. A pantograph machine devised by Bell engineers traced templates for complex machining of parts, allowing for the production of 1,200 pieces in an eight-hour shift.

High front view of XP-39E shows simplified wing root inlets. (Bell photo)

The design of the Airacobra was based on two longitudinal main beams running from the nose to the engine bay. A construction fixture held a left and right beam, to which additional angles and structure were added to flesh out the beefy lower portion of the fuselage. For the wing carry-through structure, steel members were attached to aluminum, because the steel was needed to support the demanding loads imposed at that critical location (especially because these structures have large holes for oil and prestone radiator ducting).[15]

This crucial forward fuselage assembly was the heart and soul of the Airacobra. It was, according to an analytical article in the May 1943 issue of *Aviation* magazine, the structural and philosophical focal point of the P-39 design concept. When mated with the aft section, the P-39's fuselage, including cowling and fillets, had a design weight of only 618.3 pounds. This did not include the heft of the V-1710 engine, at 1,408.5 pounds with gearbox and extension shaft. By the time engine accessories, powerplant controls, propeller and spinner, starter system, cooling system and fluid, lubricating system, and protected fuel system, were added, the powerplant in its entirety added more than 2,663 pounds to the P-39's weight. Total wing group weight was pegged at not quite 935 pounds; total vertical and horizontal tail group weight was 116 pounds. Landing gear added

P-39F followed D-model in Airacobra mass production; example photographed at Wright Field features non-standard flared exhaust stacks. (USAFM)

A P-39K photographed during refurbishing at McChord Field, Washington, in 1944 had wavy light undersurfaces atypical of most production Airacobras. (Photo by Peter M. Bowers)

P-39L has radio antenna mast behind carburetor scoop; on some Airacobras not using this style antenna mast, an airfoil-shaped flush-mounted skin plug marked the spot on the top of the fuselage. (Air Force via Bowers)

The built-up aluminum cabin doors on the P-39 had safety-glass windows that could be rolled down in flight, even at high speeds. Instead of a crank extending to one side of a window shaft mechanism, the P-39 door windows used a more compact twist handle to raise and lower the windows. In addition to the door locking mechanism on the aft edge, P-39 cabin doors were fitted with a latch at the top of the door, to keep the door from deforming out into the slipstream at high speeds.

another 516.6 pounds to the P-39 formula. Fixed equipment, to include armament provisions, communication gear, electrical equipment, surface controls, instruments, and furnishings, amounted to more than the bare fuselage, at about 674 pounds.[16]

Total empty weight of an example P-39 was 5,523.2 pounds. Useful load, figuring for a smaller pilot at 160 pounds, 104 gallons of gasoline at 624 pounds, oil, guns, ammunition, gunsight, 202.5 pounds of armor plate and nearly 60 pounds

of armor glass, was pegged at 1,880.3 pounds for an example Airacobra; operational dictates obviously created variables to this. These figures gave the typical P-39 a total aircraft weight, including useful load, of 7,403.5 pounds.[17]

A limiting landing load at gross weight was figured to be 4.67 gs — less than the dropping load expected to be tolerated by carrier-borne fighters. Limit diving speed for the P-39 was pegged at 170 percent of calibrated high speed.[18]

The cabin of the P-39 was said to be designed with an ideal pilot height of five feet, eight inches, perhaps lending credibility to the popular notion that smaller fliers became fighter pilots (although exceptions abounded). The cabin of the P-39 was an early bubble design, albeit with a total of six glazed panels and much intervening structure diminishing the clear view the pilot had. Behind the doors, a stout turnover bulkhead promised to keep the cockpit space relatively intact if the P-39 ended up inverted on the ground. This rigid turnover structure formed the shape of the cabin, and was said to be able to withstand stresses of considerably more than the Airacobra's weight.[19]

Wings of the P-39 were mounted at four degrees dihedral; airfoil at the wing root was NACA 0015; at the

P-39M (42-4770) continued basic Airacobra lines. Use of low-profile nosewheel tire with "hubcaps" is evident on this example. Mixing of accessories makes a serial number one of the few sure ways to distinguish many mid-production Airacobra variants. (Bowers collection)

An electric motor with torque tube shafts raised and lowered P-39 landing gear, as depicted in a drawing from a P-39 Erection and Maintenance manual. An emergency hand crank was built into the system in the event of electrical failure.

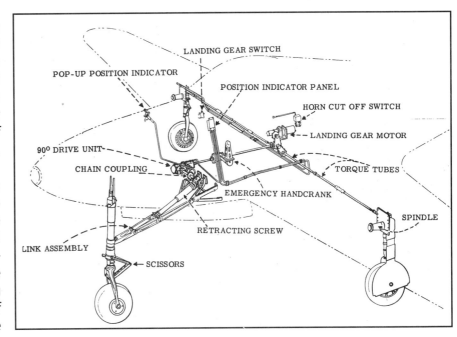

tip, it was NACA 23009. Each aileron had its own trim tab. In addition to traditional trimming chores, these aileron tabs, through a mechanical linkage, acted as servo tabs to automatically deploy opposite the movement of the aileron, imparting a force that reduced the amount of muscle required to deflect the aileron.[20]

The joining of the wing carry-through and the longitudinal beams added further strength and integrity to the whole structure. The outer wing panels bolted to the stub wing; when the wings were removed, the stub was approximately 44 inches wide, facilitating crating for overseas shipment of the Airacobra. However, this meant the main landing gear were carried in the outer wing panels, so the fuselage needed to be cradled or slung in the absence of having wings attached — sometimes an inconvenience in the field.

Another machining marvel of Airacobra construction was a Farnham milling machine designed to Bell specifications which took 13-foot rough duralumin extrusions and produced finely machined wing spar capstrips in two passes through the machine. Complex changes in material thickness, taper, and twist were handled by the milling machine in each of the two 12-minute cuts required. The outer surfaces of the spar caps were cut to allow adjacent wing skin to lap the spar cap while providing a flush surface joint between the skin and the exposed spar cap.[21]

Airacobra restorations undertaken decades after final production of P-39s have occasionally faced the prospect of replacing all of the milled capstrips, since they sometimes exhibit corrosion problems different than those of the adjoining wing skin and ribs. Latter-day costs of milling new spar caps have easily exceeded Bell's 1941 cost of about eight dollars per piece!

The P-39 was equipped with split flaps mounted at the wing trailing edges inboard of the ailerons by means of a large piano hinge running the full span of the flap. Split flaps drop the lower surface of the

P-39N-5 in the midst of overhaul that would lead to new paint shows sheetmetal rework around radio compartment hatches in aft fuselage. Other radio gear is nested in the turtle deck behind the cockpit rollover structure. This exceptionally clean inflight photo of an exceptionally scabby P-39 was taken by Peter M. Bowers on 10 June 1944 while he was an engineering officer at McChord Field, Tacoma, Washington.

Typical P-39Q (42-19549) photographed on Oahu carries a single .50-caliber machine gun beneath each wing. Bar of national insignia on lower left wing surface spills over onto machine gun pod. Wording on door reads: "Tarawa Boom Deay". (Air Force photo)

wing, while leaving the top surface fixed in place. Designed into the P-39's flaps was a calculated by-product of deflection that increased the downwash of air over the tail surfaces, making trim changes negligible from stable level cruising speed with the flaps up, right down to a stable power-off glide.[22]

Early in Airacobra production, the fabric for the movable control surfaces was stitched on by hand — a time-consuming hurdle to mass production. Bell engineers devised aluminum strips and a special tool to force the strips into grooves in the control-surface ribs, proving better at holding the fabric tight than hand stitching, and providing

time savings of as much as 50 percent in this operation.

Even with mass-production shortcut innovations devised by Bell, the construction of P-39s still had some labor-intensive handwork. Some subassemblies, like the aluminum wingtips, were clamped together with Cleco devices — temporary holders that can be spread to fill a rivet hole, and then diminished in size and extracted to allow driving the actual rivet. In this way, the wingtips could be pieced together, and then placed on a flat workbench to be riveted permanently.[23]

Landing gear was tricycle-style, with a castering but non-steerable nose-wheel on a long strut, and two shorter main gear legs, all operated electrically by means of universal joints, gear boxes, and mechanical linkages. For emergencies, a ratchet handle to the right of the pilot's seat, sprouting from the cabin floor, could be used to operate the landing gear.[24] (On P-39s, this ratchet handle device extends up from the cabin floor at approximately a right

Perhaps the first two-place TP-39Q trainer (42-20024), this example retained some of the canopy framing above the site of the original windscreen even after this was superseded by a higher Plexiglas bridge to the new front cockpit. As ungainly as the TP-39 is, it attests to the original sense of aesthetics and balance that graced single-seat P-39s. Longer dorsal fin is evident on this example; a ventral fin was also added for stability when the aerodynamics were altered by the addition of the forward cockpit in the former gun bay. This TP-39 was photographed at the salvage yard at Ontario, California, in early 1946. (Bowers collection)

angle; on P-63s, the handle is canted forward, possibly accommodating the relative difference in placement of the P-63 cabin over the wing *vice* the placement on the P-39.)

When retracted, the P-39 nose-wheel nested in a curved bump in the cockpit floor. The main gear of the P-39 were covered by a large semi-circular door and a smaller panel attached to the landing gear struts. (Two panels were used to accommodate the extension and compression of the oleo strut.) During the gear retraction cycle, the main gear tires came in contact with a spring-loaded arm on the "flipper doors" located inboard of the gear, thereby pushing on the arms to retract the flipper doors over the gear. During gear extension, the spring-loaded arms pushed the flipper doors open.[25] (Most P-63 Kingcobras were delivered without any kind of flipper door, leaving part of the main landing gear exposed when retracted.)

Six rubber fuel cells in each wing provided 120 gallons of internal gasoline tankage; the centerline bomb shackle could alternately be used to hold a drop tank. Thought was given to attaching underwing shackles to the P-39, but as a production choice, this was limited to the later P-63.

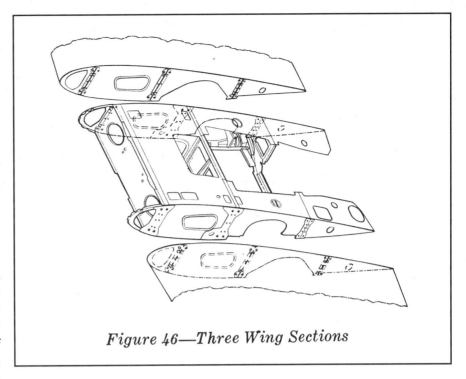

Figure 46—Three Wing Sections

Line drawing shows how Airacobra outer wing panels mated to the stub wing, which was built into the forward fuselage. Gussets on face of stub wing strengthened area where wing bolts held outer wings to center section.

The P-39 used an electric inertia starter, activated via a foot pedal on the right side of the cockpit floor. To energize the engine starter, the pedal was pushed rearward by the pilot's heel. Once the starter was sufficiently energized to cause the engine to turn over, the foot pedal was depressed forward with the toe of the pilot's shoe, to engage the starter and engine. A hand-crank for emergency inertia cranking was stowed beneath the right wing trailing edge.[26]

Airflow into the cockpit of the P-39 was at a constant rate, although its temperature could be regulated by the pilot. In theory, the constant-rate flow of air into the cockpit was

Sole XFL-1 Airabonita, fortuitously photographed with an AAF P-39 beside it, circa 1942, points up salient differences between the two aircraft, including higher Airabonita canopy and door, exposed main wheels, underwing-mounted air inlets, tailwheel, and tailhook. Problems, including nagging aft center of gravity, bedeviled the Airabonita. (Bell photograph)

XFL-1 Airabonita main wheels folded close together in the leading edge of the wing, precluding wing root inlets for oil and engine coolers; bulky underwing coolers resulted. Airabonita wing was built as a one-piece unit instead of the way P-39 wings were made up of a stub with outer panels. (Bell photo)

Side view of the XFL-1 shows some of its holdover traits from the original XP-39: High-domed cockpit and narrow vertical fin chord. But the Airabonita was vastly different than merely a warmed-over Airacobra, and included a host of Navy-mandated features including a protective center post to the windscreen to act as a cable fender in case the aircraft managed to slip an arresting cable over the top of its nose. (Bell photo)

at a higher pressure than the air in the gun bay in the nose, to cause gun fumes to remain outside the cockpit. In practice, gunpowder fumes entering the cockpit were a problem for some Airacobra pilots.

Airacobras were built at Buffalo, New York, and Niagara Falls, New York. Four parallel Airacobra assembly lines at Niagara Falls were mechanized to move in fractionalized inches each minute, propelled by subterranean chain drives to which fuselage fixtures were hooked. The first four stations on the assembly line were used to complete installation of internal fuselage components. By station five, the fuselage "canoe" was ready to receive its Allison engine; at station six, the pre-assembled pilot's cabin was installed, giving form and identity to the P-39. Station nine saw attachment of the aft fuselage. About midway through each line,

Airacobra in the making has heavy basket of armor plating bolted ahead of the critical gearbox in the nose. In addition to protecting the gearbox from frontal gunfire, this armor also sheltered the pilot several feet to the rear. A tubular opening in the forward fuselage of P-39s permitted insertion of a lifting rod to support the nose in a frame such as the one used on the assembly line. Another tube could be passed through an opening in the aft fuselage. (EAA/Dennis Parks)

horizontal tails were attached; near the end, wings were bolted on, and the mechanically-complete Airacobras were parked in staggered array on the shop floor, destined for the airfield outside.[27]

The Buffalo assembly plant, on which many export Airacobras intended for Britain were built in 1941, did not have mechanized movement.

As production quantities increased, efficiencies generally led to a lower unit cost per P-39. USAAF statistics place the average cost of a P-39 approved during fiscal years 1939-1941 at $77,159. By 1942, this was down to $69,534, and by 1944, the unit cost of a P-39 was pegged at $50,666. By contrast, a P-51 Mustang cost less than a thousand dollars more than a P-39 by 1944, with the Mustang's unit price at $51,572. The hefty turbosupercharged P-47 Thunderbolt remained costlier throughout the war, posting a unit price of $104,258 for 1943 and still $85,578 for 1944. Low price leader was the rugged, if outdated, P-40, coming in at $44,892 for fiscal 1944.[28]

AIRABONITA: A FORGETTABLE FOOTNOTE

The Bell Aircraft Corporation penchant for innovation, and enthusiasm for engaging new ideas and projects, was a vignette of the brash optimism that characterized American capitalists in that less-restrictive era. With the P-39 still very much a developmental pre-production project and the twin-engine Airacuda bomber destroyer a small run, the young aircraft manufacturing company yearned for more contracts, and yet had limited capital to invest in nurturing new projects.

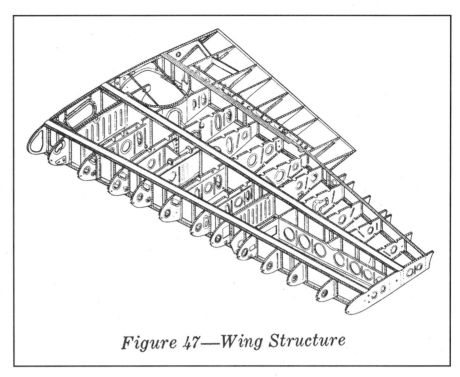

Figure 47—Wing Structure

Airacobra outer wing panels, as depicted in the Erection and Maintenance manual, were built up of stamped ribs and structure mated to milled spar caps, and then skinned in aluminum.

P-39Ds supported by dollies near completion on the Bell line. Early .30-caliber wing gun installations such as these allowed the gun's perforated cooling jacket to project from the wing; later .30-caliber P-39 wing guns were shrouded in larger diameter stainless steel tubes attached to a leading edge plate that could be removed for servicing. (EAA/Dennis Parks)

Dual rows of Airacobra fuselages receive attention at the Bell factory. Three-blade propellers are stacked on edge in crates to the right. (EAA/Dennis Parks)

Business end of the Airacobra was the form-fitting M-4 37-MM cannon and magazine, atop the extension drive shaft, all of which mated to the gearbox immediately behind the propeller. This example was displayed at the U.S. Air Force Museum in Dayton, Ohio, beside the museum's P-39Q.

In the late 1930s, the U.S. Navy was formulating ideas for its next fighter aircraft. The Navy, for a variety of reasons, had always adhered to the use of air-cooled radial engines for its shipboard aircraft. Radials were considered highly reliable and rugged, easier to service in the cramped surroundings of an aircraft carrier, and less demanding on the supplies and materials that had to be carried on shipboard for their servicing and operation, since they did not have a closed-circuit liquid cooling system.

Lockheed, with innovator Kelly Johnson, tried without success to interest the Navy in a carrier-borne version of its Allison-engined P-38. Lockheed drawings exist showing a radial-engined variant of the P-38 for Navy operations, but neither came to be.[29] In fact, the Navy's zone of comfort for fighter procurement was in the realm of several east-coast manufacturers of radial-engine warplanes: Vought, Grumman, Brewster, and Curtiss. In 1938, Bell Aircraft addressed a Navy request for single-engine fighter proposals by offering what, at least superficially, looked like a modified XP-39 with a tailwheel.

But the Airabonita, as Bell called its Navy offering, demanded far more than a relocated landing gear and a tailhook to become a viable shipboard warplane. The problems encountered in developing the

Airabonita were compounding and confounding. To make the navalized "P-39" (given U.S. Navy designation XFL-1) sit properly on its tailwheel, the mainwheels had to be moved forward to put more pivoting weight aft. This altered the way the wheels fit into the wings, and resulted in a one-piece wing for the Airabonita instead of outer panels bolted to a center stub. The one-piece construction limited the ability to bury cooling ducts and radiators in the center section. Originally, Bell planned to mount the oil cooler on the right side of the fuselage and the engine cooler on the left, but these were relocated to underwing locations, with some attendant overheating problems.

Bowing to a Navy request that now seems painfully inappropriate, Bell engineers put five small doors on the underside of each wing, closeting five small bomb bays per side, in which to carry bombs that were to be dropped over enemy aircraft formations in flight. Other navalized features of the era included flotation bags in the wings that could deploy to keep the Airabonita afloat in the event of a ditching. And of course, the landing gear and other structure had to be stressed to withstand the higher sink rates and abruptly-arrested carrier landings.

The Navy rejected Bell's plan to use the 37-MM cannon in the nose, opting instead for a 23-MM weapon and two .30-caliber machine guns, or, one .50-caliber machine gun and two .30-calibers. All of the

Erection and Maintenance manual drawing of Airacobra right outer wing panel shows bolt hole locations; cutouts for oil and glycol cooler ducts routed into center wing stub.

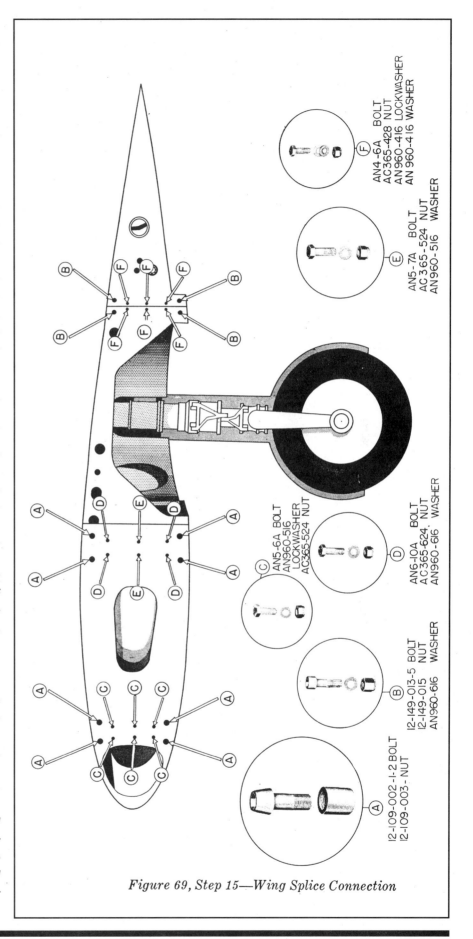

Figure 69, Step 15—Wing Splice Connection

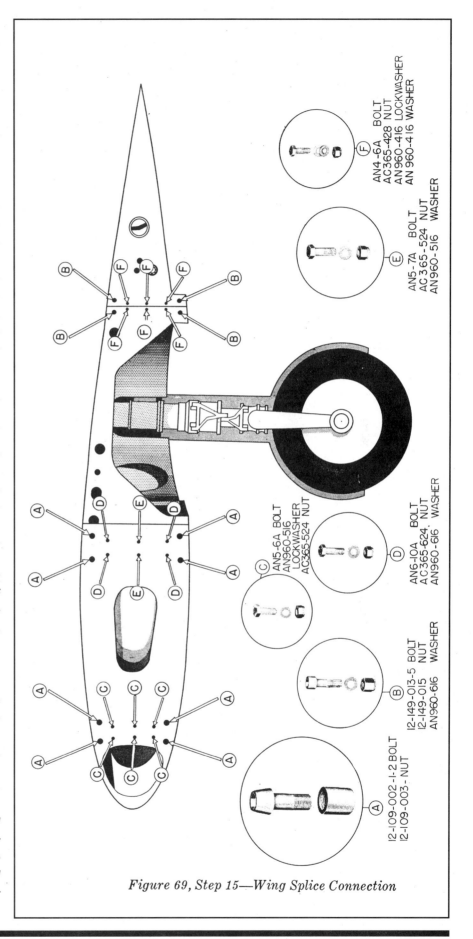

P-39M cockpit photo reveals instrument panel details. Throttle at left impedes quick exit from the left door, making the right door the favored exit for bailouts. The .50-caliber machine guns are not installed in this example. N-3 gunsight at top center of panel has rubber crash pad to protect pilot. (USAFM)

assumptions and revisions wrapped up in the development of the XFL-1 Airabonita, including the scaling back of the size of the nose armament, had one outcome: An already aft-located center of gravity became ever more so, as the nose was lightened and the tail made heavier with a tailwheel and arresting hook.

At one point in the design phase, Bell engineers were split over the desirability of relocating the Airabonita's wing farther back to alleviate the aft center of gravity problem. But, for whatever reasons, this was not done, and the engineers had to put their faith in other means of restoring a viable center of gravity to the XFL-1.[30]

Bell Aircraft submitted the proposal which led to the construction of the Airabonita in April 1938. First flight was more than two years later, on 13 May 1940. It was delivered to the Navy after company test flights, on 26 February 1941, and underwent Navy acceptance trials from March through September of that year before quietly slipping away as little more than an anecdote in the history of Bell Aircraft.[31]

P-39L cockpit photo is instructive for several reasons: drive shaft cover can be seen at bottom center of photo, leading up to boot around base of control stick. Portion of landing gear ratchet handle is visible to the right of control stick boot. Elevator trim wheel is at left of photo. Twist knob for rolling down side window is visible in lefthand cockpit door. Original purpose for this photo was to show switch installation near bottom of door for reconnaissance cameras installed on this aircraft in the summer of 1942. (USAFM)

The Airabonita was a mixed blessing. It had the high-domed cockpit canopy reminiscent of the prototype XP-39; while this provided good pilot visibility for carrier operations, wind tunnel tests showed

Mock-up installation of ventrally-mounted cameras in a test P-39L included a vertical K-24 and rear oblique K-25 camera. [Some other camera mods seen on P-39s in the Pacific put cameras in openings in the side radio compartment hatches]. (USAFM)

marked improvements in drag would result from lowering this structure even a few inches. The landlocked P-39 underwent such a canopy reduction; it was felt the Airabonita could not. But most damning of all was the aft center of gravity, that could only be brought into a reasonable state by ballasting the nose compartment — not a viable option for a combat aircraft.

So many decades after the XFL-1 was built, it is left to speculation why Bell did not rein in the runaway center-of-gravity problem when it was first suspected. But the Airabonita did not see production or service, and Allison engines did not serve the U.S. Navy.

The second P-400 export Airacobra built, number AH571, was groomed by Bell for speed trials in which it attained 391 miles an hour. Modifications include non-standard rudder, fairing around special exhaust stacks, and lack of the usual ram air inlet ahead of the exhaust stacks for spark plug cooling. Noticeable also is the omission of the overhead canopy retaining strip, which apparently varied on P-400s and P-39Cs. (Bell photo via Peter M. Bowers.)

---

[1] "The Victorious Vees," by Pat Plummer, *Wings* magazine, Aug. 1997. [2] Alain J. Pelletier, *Bell Aircraft Since 1935*, Naval Institute Press, Annapolis, Maryland, 1992. [3] For a lengthy documented discussion of the decision to remove turbosupercharging from the Airacobra, see also Birch Matthews' *Cobra! Bell Aircraft Corporation, 1934-1946*, Schiffer Publishing, Atglen, Pennsylvania, 1996. [4] Alain J. Pelletier, *Bell Aircraft Since 1935*, Naval Institute Press, Annapolis, Maryland, 1992. [5] Birch Matthews, *Cobra! Bell Aircraft Corporation — 1934-1946*, Schiffer, Atglen, Pennsylvania, 1996. [6] "Aircraft Equipment Chart" for P-39 models, produced as a maintenance aid by Bell Aircraft Corp. during World War Two. [7] Alain J. Pelletier, *Bell Aircraft Since 1935*, Naval Institute Press, Annapolis, Maryland, 1992. [8] "Index of AF Serial Numbers Assigned to Aircraft 1958 and Prior", Procurement Division, Programmed Procurement Branch, Reports Section (USAF). [9] Alain J. Pelletier, *Bell Aircraft Since 1935*, Naval Institute Press, Annapolis, Maryland, 1992. [10] "Aircraft Equipment Chart" for P-39 models, produced as a maintenance aid by Bell Aircraft Corp. during World War Two. [11] USAAF Tactical Planning Characteristics and Performance Chart, as of 23 February 1945. [12] "Design Analysis of the Bell Airacobra From Cannon to Tail," by E. Eugene Miller, *Aviation* magazine, May 1943. [13] "How Airacobras are Built," by O.L. Woodson, *American Machinist* magazine, 12 November 1941. [14] *Ibid.* [15] *Ibid.* [16] "Design Analysis of the Bell Airacobra From Cannon to Tail," by E. Eugene Miller, *Aviation* magazine, May 1943. [17] *Ibid.* [18] *Ibid.* [19] *Ibid.* [20] *Ibid.* [21] "How Airacobras are Built," by O.L. Woodson, *American Machinist* magazine, 12 November 1941. [22] *Ibid.* [23] *Ibid.* [24] *Ibid.* [25] "Design Analysis of the Bell Airacobra From Cannon to Tail," by E. Eugene Miller, *Aviation* magazine, May 1943. [26] *Ibid.* [27] "How Airacobras are Built," by O.L. Woodson, *American Machinist* magazine, 12 November 1941. [28] *Army Air Forces Statistical Digest — World War II —* USAAF HQ, Office of Statistical Control, December 1945. [29] For more on the theoretical naval variants of the P-38, see WarbirdTech Volume 2, *Lockheed P-38 Lightning*, by the author. [30] Birch Matthews, *Cobra! Bell Aircraft Corporation — 1934-1946*, Schiffer, Atglen, Pennsylvania, 1996. [31] *Ibid.*

THE MECHANICS OF WAR

A cadre of Bell technical representatives arrived in England beginning in October 1942 to oversee the modification of P-400s (as export Airacobras originally intended for Britain were known) and assembly of new P-39Ls and Ms destined for combat with USAAF units in North Africa. Their periodic dispatches back to Bell headquarters provided insights into the Airacobra's care and feeding. Early on, the Bell tech reps oversaw the installation of carburetor air filters — signaling the intended departure of these Airacobras for the North African desert.

Early in the program, during October 1942, Bell rep Raymond Sebring related a mishap that had incredible results for the pilot of one of the British Airacobras (serial BX 418) being modified for USAAF use: "Almost immediately after landing a two-and-a-half-ton truck pulled across the end of the runway on the perimeter track and the plane hit it head on demolishing both plane and truck. Due to rigid construction of our [Airacobra cockpit] cabin and nose section Lieutenant Niban [the pilot] was not hurt other than a slight cut on the head and a bruise near the left eye. Luckily the truck driver was thrown out of the truck by the crash and escaped with body bruises and a broken leg."[1]

By November the tech reps in England were involved in attaching a centerline bomb shackle to Airacobras, capable of carrying a range-extending fuel tank. Also on their list of projects was assisting in the assembly of 76 new P-39Ls that arrived crated from the U.S. Bell representative John Baughman noted that the new L-models "are also being camouflaged like P400 units", probably referring to a two-tone top coat seen on some later USAAF Airacobras in North Africa.[2] Not all multi-hue P-39s were exactly the same shades as P-400s, according to some published references.

With the shackles installed beneath P-400s and P-39Ls, the Bell representatives performed a landing gear retraction on a blocked example of both models of the Airacobra, noting frequent contacts between the nosewheel and the seam flange on the large 150-gallon ferry tank. P-400s had nosewheel tire contact with the tanks in 45 percent of the aircraft; this was reduced to 25 percent with the tested L-models. Rather than keep trimming flanges, a Bell representative suggested moving the attach lugs on the drop tanks forward three-fourths of an inch; if this would cause center-of-gravity problems, then reducing flange width at the nose of the tank from 1-5/8 to 1-1/8 inches was urged.[3]

Early Airacobra drop tanks lacked baffling sufficient to keep fuel from sloshing, and a Bell representative reported on 7 December 1942: "I have had considerable complaint on the belly tanks as regards flight characteristics when about half of the fuel has been consumed. The tank obviously needs longitudinal

V-1710 engine nested right behind pilot's seat in the P-39. Small bump on outside of fuselage beneath rollover structure, and just ahead of exhaust stacks, is ram air scoop to cool spark plugs. The Airacobra came apart with many removable cowlings and turtle deck pieces to access the engine and gun bays. (USAFM)

baffles in order to prevent sid[e]sway of gasoline and consequent wallowing of the ship in flight."[4]

Bell tech rep John R. Baughman wrote late in November 1942 that the Airacobras at his base were operating well, albeit at the hands of some green pilots who were not used to the intricacies of the fighter: "A few of the boys did not have much time in our units (the Bell tech reps referred to Airacobras as "units") and they bent three nose wheel forks."[5]

On the last day of November 1942, Bell representative C.J. O'Connor, Jr., reported the P-400s being groomed for combat assignment to North Africa were nearing completion. Using a rudimentary code to avoid giving specific numbers of aircraft in his communication, O'Connor said: "We have just twice my age [number of P-400s] to do here at this Base. Remote compass installation is the only item which has to be done on these aircraft. All the other modifications are now completed in every P.400 aircraft." The compass problem which the British had earlier noted was being rectified. After cracking front windscreens in about a dozen Airacobras in England, the Bell representatives turned to local manufacture after their source of spares was depleted. Tech rep O'Connor

With carburetor scoop, other cowlings, and cowl stiffeners removed, mechanics steady a P-39 Allison engine as it is changed on a combat-veteran Airacobra of the 110th Tactical Reconnaissance Squadron of the 71st Tactical Reconnaissance Group at Tadji, New Guinea, on 27 August 1944. (Air Force photo)

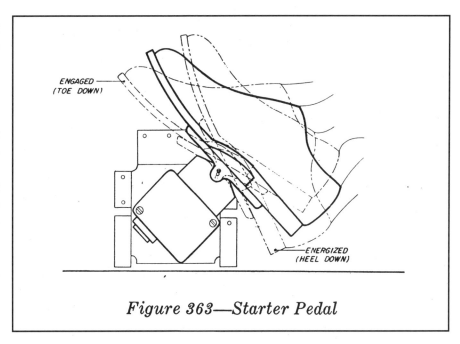

Figure 363—Starter Pedal

Foot pedal for starting the Airacobra was explained by this drawing in a P-39 manual. A hand crank was stowed aboard the aircraft for emergency ground starting.

explained: "I have informed all foremen to tell the men that they should not sit on that front armor plate, which is mounted on the front windscreen. Especially the armament gang, when taking out or installing the .50-cal. guns and cannon they have a habit of sitting on this armor plate and as a result the front windscreen cracks."[6]

The dampness of England combined with periods of inactivity for the Airacobras awaiting combat

Spray cleaning the underside of a P-39 at Ephrata Army Airfield, Washington, was captured in an Air Force photograph that reveals details of the landing gear doors. As the main wheels retracted, they pushed a rod on the inboard "flipper doors," which closed over the edge of the main wheel doors.

assignments, causing ignition problems in the Allison engines. Bell technicians, aided by two Allison representatives, traced the problem to two sources: "The main trouble was... excessive sweating in the distributor cases. This was caused by the very damp and cold weather during which the ships were necessarily parked outside. After thoroughly drying the cases, the ships would be flown and would function very well. The next time they were flown however the same missing and roughness would occur." The Bell representatives learned the moisture had returned between flights. "Finally we gave the distributor covers a treatment of oil and while this did not entirely eliminate the moisture, we had considerably less trouble. All ships will be given a thorough drying just before final takeoff and there is no doubt but what they will function well in this respect during their trip" [to their combat location, or "extended service" as the Bell technicians called it in their reports.] During fuel consumption calibration flights — a necessity for aircraft planning long missions such as ferry flights, since no two machines were truly alike — the crews learned "that by clearing the engine through occasional use of take-off RPM and manifold pressure for a period of five or ten seconds, a much smoother running engine was obtained. This also seemed to have very little bearing on fuel consumption."[7]

As the Bell representatives overcame problems, new ones arose. The recently assembled P-39Ls were fraught with malfunctions in the 37-MM cannon, with empty shells rattling around and catching on the mechanism instead of ejecting cleanly. The technicians tried a couple remedies including stretching a wire across part of the chute mechanism to keep shells from rebounding. While this appeared to

A tied-down Airacobra test fires its entire complement of .30-caliber, .50-caliber, and 37-millimeter guns with its engine running. Muzzle flash from the nose guns was of some concern. (Peter M. Bowers collection)

Airacobra "Dash-2" Erection and Maintenance manual artwork shows inboard leading edge inlets were for the coolant radiator ducting; outboard inlets serviced the oil coolers. Outlets for these systems were ventrally located.

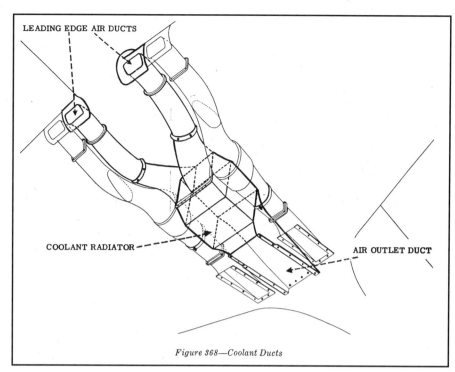

Figure 368—Coolant Ducts

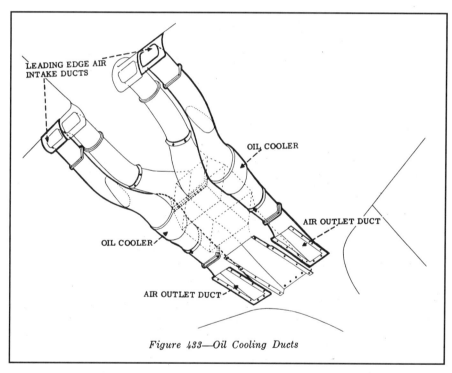

Figure 433—Oil Cooling Ducts

work, it was hardly an operational fix, but rather an indication of the nature of the problem. Other L-models were fixed by bending a deflector plate to ensure the empty shell could not travel in the way of the mechanism.[8] This seemed to help substantially. Subsequent reports indicated the jamming improved itself on a number of Airacobras after firing the guns sufficiently to break-in the new mechanism[9]; still further testing suggested some cannons were serviced with the wrong grade oil, allowing firing at a speed that induced jamming.[10] The troubleshooting offered several intelligent options for fixing the problem before these Airacobras went to war.

The sturdiness of the Airacobra again paid off just before Christmas 1942 when P-400 number AHD 597 wiped out its landing gear on a mound of earth as a pilot who was just checking out in the Airacobra attempted a landing. According to Bell representative Raymond Sebring: "…the plane finally landed on the nose and was wrecked beyond repair. The pilot was not injured beyond a slight cut on the head."[11]

Of interest was a note by Bell technician Irving Rix on the serviceability of new P-39Ls versus the P-400s in his care in the UK in late December 1942: "The 'L' models have had very few maintenance troubles other than normal radio etc. The 400s seem to have more leaks, ill-fitting cowlings, etc., to contend with. All are in service however and in general are in very good condition." Perhaps this reflected increased experience at the Bell factory, making the newer P-39Ls more trouble free, or maybe it was age on the P-400s. Rix did not offer his opinion on the cause.[12]

As the Airacobras in England were readied for combat in North Africa, to include ground attack duties, a Bell technician noted on 7 January 1943: "In the past few days we have been installing armor plating under the pilots seats. This seems to be very desirable and very easily installed. The procedure is to bolt

Looking like an assembly line, a major overhaul project for weary Airacobras was undertaken at a sub-depot at McChord Field, Washington, in 1944. As many as 26 P-39s a month were refurbished in this way. The photo shows a variety of paint schemes, including a stripped metal P-39 which still retained the original colors on its fabric control surfaces when the photo was taken. (USAAF photo)

the plate to the bottom of the seat. The plate is cut to the same size as the bottom of the seat." No doubt this particular armor installation location was a morale booster for Airacobra pilots. The separate, internally-bolted armor glass in the front windscreen of Airacobras was a dirt trap that was time consuming to clean. Bell representative Irving Rix said: "The pilots are all of the opinion that the front armor glass should be incorporated in the construction of the front wind shield to the end that visibility would be improved and it would also facilitate cleaning."[13] [Such a one-piece front armored windscreen was introduced on the P-63 Kingcobra.]

After early ferry flights of Airacobras from the UK to North Africa included some diversions to Spain and Portugal when some of the aircraft ran low on fuel, a depot-level project began in England to mount a pair of additional 75-gallon fuel tanks, one under each wing, on Airacobras before sending them away. When Bell technical representatives learned of this idea, they quickly informed the AAF about a 300-gallon centerline tank being tested on a P-39 instead. Work stopped on the notion of wing-mounted tanks on Airacobras, although this was a feature on P-63 Kingcobras.[14]

A 200-gallon auxiliary fuel tank was available for testing on a P-39 in England by January 1943. Similar to the 150-gallon tank, only wider, the new device was made of automobile body-type steel. To test han-

For a 1944 war bond parade through the streets of Tacoma, Washington, a young engineering officer at McChord Field by the name of Peter M. Bowers took a P-39 that belly-landed at McChord and was due to be scrapped, and "decorated" it with bullet holes from a sub-machine gun he checked out. The resulting tableau was trailered through town with a banner proclaiming: "Earn as you Learn — Clover Park School Trains Workers for McChord". (Air Force photo via Carl Schuler)

Gearbox in the nose of the P-39 had its own oil reservoir. Drive shaft connected low on the box; gears transmitted power to the propeller shaft, which was hollow to accommodate a cannon.

dling characteristics with the 200-gallon tank when empty, it was taken aloft under an Airacobra, exhibiting no unusual flight characteristics on takeoff. In flight, the pilot noticed no change in medium turns, but above 30 degrees of bank an abnormal rudder reaction with skidding and mushing was noted. Cruising, the Airacobra posted 165 miles an hour indicated airspeed at 1,500 feet altitude with the tank. Partial flap lowering improved climb and turn characteristics, but lowered cruising speed by 20 miles an hour.[15]

SUGGESTIONS FROM THE FIELD

An AAF summary of comments from P-39 mechanics in the field revealed quirks of the Airacobra. The items gathered in the summary were not universal or final; some might later have received sanctioning as technical orders or directives, while others were atypical. At one base, "a P-39 returned after making one turn around the field because the coolant temperature was 150 degrees Centigrade. Investigation disclosed that a tail cover was in the cooler duct and on removal the coolant temperature returned to normal. To prevent recurrence, pillows that fit the ducts have been made and with these tied together there is no possibility of taking off before removing them."[16]

Elsewhere, one cause of slight or partial engine cut-out at altitude was traced to carburetor intake scoops that were "dented on

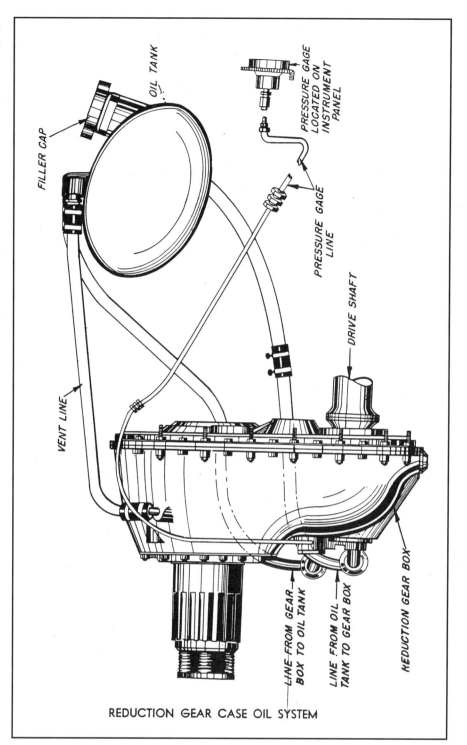

REDUCTION GEAR CASE OIL SYSTEM

removal through careless handling. They are dented at the end which meets the seal and this allows an escape of rammed air at this point. This opening also causes a burble of intake air rather than a smooth flow."[17] Clearly, the maintenance of a machine as complex as a fighter aircraft required finesse and care.

During cold-weather testing of a P-39, "it was found that engine operation was greatly improved when regular 100 octane fuel was used instead of aromatic fuel. Use of the 100 octane fuel smoothed the engine operation." All such suggestions in the document were for informational purposes and were

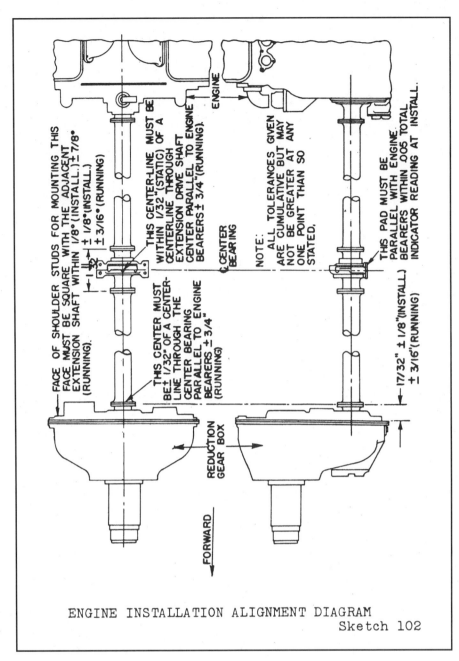

FACE OF SHOULDER STUDS FOR MOUNTING THIS FACE MUST BE SQUARE WITH THE ADJACENT EXTENSION SHAFT WITHIN 1/8" (INSTALL.) ± 7/8" (RUNNING).

± 1/8" (INSTALL.)
± 3/16" (RUNNING)

THIS CENTER-LINE MUST BE WITHIN 1/32" (STATIC) OF A CENTERLINE THROUGH EXTENSION DRIVE SHAFT CENTER PARALLEL TO ENGINE BEARERS ± 3/4" (RUNNING).

ENGINE

NOTE: ALL TOLERANCES GIVEN ARE CUMULATIVE BUT MAY NOT BE GREATER AT ANY ONE POINT THAN SO STATED.

CENTER BEARING

THIS PAD MUST BE PARALLEL WITH ENGINE BEARERS WITHIN .005 TOTAL INDICATOR READING AT INSTALL.

THIS CENTER MUST BE ± 1/32" OF A CENTER-LINE THROUGH THE CENTER BEARING PARALLEL TO ENGINE BEARERS ± 3/4" (RUNNING)

17/32" ± 1/8" (INSTALL) ± 3/16" (RUNNING)

REDUCTION GEAR BOX

FORWARD

ENGINE INSTALLATION ALIGNMENT DIAGRAM
Sketch 102

Close tolerances for alignment of the multi-piece P-39 drive line were indicated in a technical drawing which simultaneously depicted top and side views. Bell technicians found a certain amount of twisting occurred in the long drive shaft under load.

"not to be regarded as a directive or Technical Order."[18] Still, they allowed P-39 ground crews to share a common data base, and compare notes and opinions about their aircraft.

The P-39Q came in for a few complaints at one base. "The two main objections were the substitution of armor plate for the aft armor glass and the installation of one underslung .50-caliber machine gun in place of two .30-caliber machine guns in each wing. Flying personnel agreed that the Q-model did not have the aileron response nor the speed which the N-model possessed." Seemingly small things could have a big impact on performance, as reported by one Airacobra base: "In an altitude test of P-39Q-1 and Q-5 airplanes at one base, only about 20 percent would attain an altitude of over 25,000 feet. At that altitude violent backfiring and cutting-out was encountered." A check of one of the offending aircraft showed its magneto points were about a half-inch off setting and lightly pitted; a fine coat of oil was on both distributor caps; nearly-new spark plugs had gaps of

Possibly as an alternative to the onerous task of stripping the paint from Airacobras, this P-39K, seen at McChord Field in 1944, was painted aluminum silver. Curiously, the tail numbering looks like the unusual style applied at the Bell factory. (Photo by Peter M. Bowers)

Retainer strips held three-piece P-39 windscreen in place. Armor plate was bolted on the outside, lower than the internally-mounted armor glass inside the windscreen (not visible in drawing). Tube structure seen in the drawing inside the windscreen formed basis for gunsight mount.

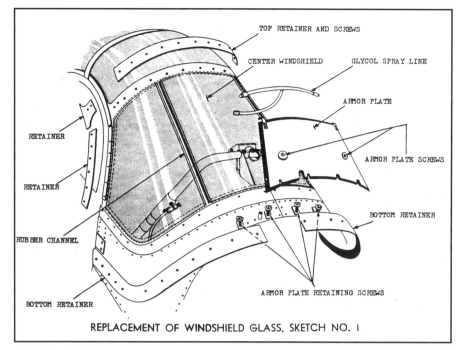

REPLACEMENT OF WINDSHIELD GLASS, SKETCH NO. 1

.015" to .016". To correct these problems, new magneto points were set with a timing disc, new rotor fingers were installed, spark plugs were correctly gapped to between .011" and .013", and the distributor caps were washed of their oil film — which seemed to be the biggest part of the original problem. "The airplane then climbed to an altitude of 33,600 feet," according to the AAF summary.[19]

One base reported Airacobra "windshield panels have been warping, bulging outward, and then blowing away in flight. It is assumed that this condition results from direct sunlight on tightly closed cabins coupled with the immediate cooling effect of sudden showers. As a temporary repair, bolts have been inserted in the panels with large washers on each side. In most cases this results in cracking of both the center glass and the sides. The best repair is a cap strip of .062" dural about 3/4-inch wide, bolted at one-inch spacing. A thin rubber padding is inserted beneath each strip."[20]

One can only speculate whether this would have any bearing on the crash of the racer Cobra I in 1946 (see Chapter Eight of this volume).

In April 1944, the 46th Fighter Squadron wrote to the Air Service Command at Patterson Field about rough-running engines in P-39Qs of different block numbers: "This malfunction has been very noticeable

Another of the 1944 war bond floats devised by Peter M. Bowers included a smaller scale Zero at the front of a trailer, rocked and banked by a worker concealed in the "Mount Fuji" beneath the aircraft, seemingly pursued by a freshly-painted P-39Q. The Airacobra actually was without its engine, and with exhaust stacks dummied in place. A small McChord Field worker was closeted in the engine bay, Bowers recalled, where a hand crank attached to the drive line permitted him to turn the propeller while a pilot in the P-39 cockpit fired blanks as the "Zero" up

front emitted carbon dioxide "smoke". Bowers later said that his imaginative Airacobra floats were well-received along the parade route, but the mayor's trophy for best float was given to a standard GI truck filled with bathing beauties from the nearby ordnance depot! Bowers called this "the triumph of sex over technology."

Stripped aluminum finish P-39D-2-BE (41-38484), nicknamed Daisy Mae, was photographed on PSP matting in a tropical locale. Wing and upper cowl machine guns have been deleted; 20-MM cannon is in nose. (Bowers collection)

on all of the P-39Q-20s. After a flight, the pilot would report the engine operating very roughly. By talking to the pilot we would find that he had operated at RPMs below 2000 for as much as 15 minutes, which would load the engine and foul the spark plugs. It has been found a better practice to operate the engine at RPMs as nearly as possible to 2150. This gives the engine a chance to stay cleaner, and… the spark plugs do not foul as quickly at this setting." The squadron caught on to the problem when flying newer P-39Q-20s in formation with older P-39Q-1s, which had a comparable manifold pressure. What the squadron deduced was: "The aerodynamic forces on the P-39Q-20 are less than the ones on the P-39(Q)-1 because of the rough spots on the wings of the old airplanes.

This makes for a smaller driving force to pull the Q-20 along in the air. This is the reason that low RPMs were necessary on the later airplanes when in flight, than with the airplanes that had been in service for as much as 369:45 hours", wrote civilian technical representative B. Corlew.[21]

Examples of technical feedback on P-39 operations make one thing clear: Dedicated technical representatives and mechanics leaned forward to meet any challenges sent their way by the fortunes of war, and by their compact Airacobra fighters.

Even this P-39Q-5 (42-20407) received a mottled camouflage scheme with light wavy undersurfaces, not typical for production Airacobra colors. (E.M. Sommerich via Bowers)

[1] Report No. 2, Bell technical representative Raymond Sebring to A.L. Fornoff, Bell Aircraft service division manager, 24 October 1942. [2] Report No. 3, Bell technical representative (name missing) to A.L. Fornoff, Bell Aircraft service division manager, 22 November 1942. [3] Ibid. [4] Report (not numbered), Bell technical representative Irving H. Rix to A.L. Fornoff, Bell Aircraft service division manager, 7 December 1942. [5] Report No. 5, Bell technical representative John R. Baughman to A.L. Fornoff, Bell Aircraft service division manager, 25 November 1942. [6] Report No. 5, Bell technical representative C.J. O'Connor, Jr. to A.L. Fornoff, Bell Aircraft service division manager, 30 November 1942. [7] Report No. 6, Bell technical representative Raymond Sebring to A.L. Fornoff, Bell Aircraft service division manager, 11 December 1942. [8] Report No. 7, Bell technical representative Irving H. Rix to A.L. Fornoff, Bell Aircraft service division manager, 19 December 1942. [9] Report No. 9, Bell technical representative Raymond Sebring to A.L. Fornoff, Bell Aircraft service division manager, 2 January 1943. [10] Report No. 10, Bell technical representative Irving H. Rix to A.L. Fornoff, Bell Aircraft service division manager, 7 January 1943. [11] Report (not numbered), Bell technical representative Raymond Sebring to A.L. Fornoff, Bell Aircraft service division manager, 25 December 1942. [12] Report No. 8, Bell technical representative Irving H. Rix to A.L. Fornoff, Bell Aircraft service division manager, 26 December 1942. [13] Report No. 10, Bell technical representative Irving H. Rix to A.L. Fornoff, Bell Aircraft service division manager, 7 January 1943. [14] Technical Report No. 10, Bell technical representative John R. Baughman to A.L. Fornoff, Bell Aircraft Corp. service manager, 25 January 1943. [15] Technical Report (not numbered), Bell technical representative (copy unsigned) to A.L. Fornoff, Bell Aircraft Corp. service manager, 28 February 1943. [16] *A Summary of Comments, Recommendations, and Experiences in the Field as Affecting the P-39*, Training Intelligence Reports 500-1500, Digest No. 4, Training Intelligence Service, Army Air Forces Training Command, Chanute Field, Illinois (undated). [17] Ibid. [18] Ibid. [19] Ibid. [20] Ibid. [21] Letter, Mr. B. Corlew, Technical Representative, to Commanding General, Air Service Command, Patterson Field, Fairfield, Ohio, Subject: "Weekly Report from APO #959, 46th Fighter Squadron", 14 April 1944.

P-63 DESIGN & DEVELOPMENT

KINGCOBRA ADVANCED THE ART

Conceived in peacetime 1941 and first flown in 1942, the Bell P-63 Kingcobra was the last piston-engine fighter designed for the U.S. Army Air Forces to go into mass production, albeit most were ultimately exported to other nations. Bell Aircraft Corporation engineers availed themselves of the technical information provided by the National Advisory Committee for Aeronautics (NACA), in whose wind tunnel at Langley, Virginia, the original XP-39 had been tested and found wanting. Initial outgrowths of the Bell-NACA relationship included a general clean-up of the XP-39 air-

frame. The XP-39E represented a number of aerodynamic changes, excluding laminar-flow technology, that resulted. A push to embrace promising new laminar-flow airfoil technology took on a life of its own, even before the XP-39E flew; on 27 June 1941, the USAAF ordered two prototypes of a laminar-flow fighter

from Bell under the new designation XP-63. The P-63 became the vehicle with which to explore and produce innovations beyond the scope of the P-39.

In about 1943, the U.S. Office of War Information released a limited amount of information about the

Bell founder Lawrence Bell (left) and two others posed for a Bell publicity photo beside that company's "10,000th Fighter Plane", as proclaimed by the banner. The aircraft is a P-63 with a Soviet red star insignia on the aft fuselage encircled by a white disc.

The XP-63A (42-78015) displayed an error in serial number application when this photo was taken; numerals on its tail should read 278015; the 2 was deleted. The turtledeck Plexiglas windows have been replaced with aluminum panels to block light, allowing for even illumination from artificial lights, to permit photography of test instrumentation mounted in that area. This early pre-production Kingcobra still had flipper doors for the main landing gear, a feature usually omitted on P-63s. Shape of underwing gun pod changed later.

P-63A with ventral fin normally associated with C-models and later. (Sommerich via Bowers)

P-63 to the press, characterizing it simply for its "long wing and two-stage Allison supercharged engine" optimistically said to make the airplane a viable contender as high as 40,000 feet above the earth.[1]

Damage to one of the XP-63s put a halt to testing in January 1943, and the second prototype, first flown in February, crashed in May of 1943. A third aircraft, the XP-63A which had been ordered in June 1942, first flew on 26 April 1943.

With an aerodynamically advanced design, the P-63 also capitalized on Allison advances in two-stage mechanical superchargers that promised to make up for the lack in altitude performance of earlier Allisons without turbos, and which had powered the P-39 Airacobra with only a single-stage mechanical supercharger.[2] The P-63's success at altitude was as much a triumph for Allison as it was for Bell. The two-stage supercharger provided sufficient masses of air for fuel combustion at higher altitudes where a single-stage unit was inadequate.

Tenth production P-63A shows lack of main gear flipper doors, plus revised wing gun pod shape. Photo taken at Wright Field in June 1946. (Peter M. Bowers)

A pair of Kingcobras used by the British to test the durability of laminar flow technology in service suggested the highly-touted special airfoil shape could be easily and substantially degraded by routine abrasions and nicks sustained in operations. Even bugs smashed against the leading edge could upset the airflow enough to reduce its laminar traits, suggesting other features were more to credit for the outstanding performance of the P-63, and of the P-51 Mustang, for that matter. Limitations to precision

Bubble-topped P-63D did not lead to production of this variant. Typical Bell use of armor glass behind pilot to allow rear vision is evident in this photo. (Bell via Bowers)

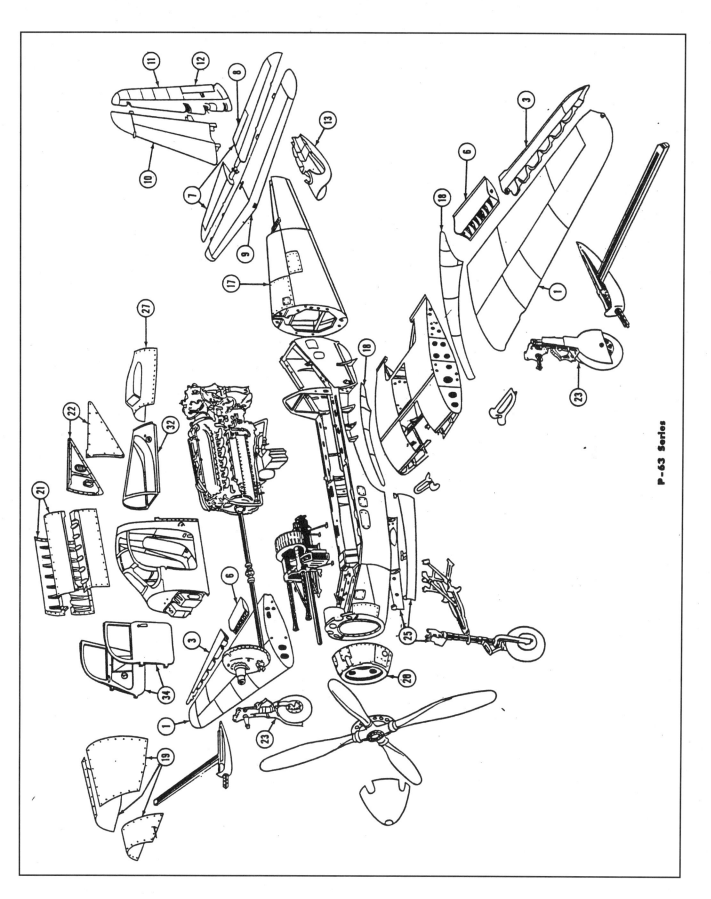

Exploded diagram of P-63A shows some construction similarities to the P-39, but most components were of new design. Kingcobra gun bay cowling arrangement differed from that of P-39. (Bill Miranda collection)

P-63E (43-11720) resumed use of ventral fin, and used large oval carburetor inlet similar to P-39 inlet, and different from squared inlet seen on P-63As. (Bell via Bowers)

Sculpted tall tail of the P-63F only adorned the only two examples of this model. Opaque aft canopy may be presumed to contain instrumentation and recording cameras with their own light source. (Bell via Bowers)

in construction methods of the era probably precluded adherence to a truly viable laminar flow wing during World War Two.[3]

A New Airplane

The Kingcobra's undeniable descendancy from the P-39 Airacobra has led to a common perception that the P-63 was a hashed-up design that used a lot of common P-39 parts. In reality, very few P-39 parts interchange with the P-63. From the outset, a different airfoil and greater span made the P-63 wing all-new; the planform of all of the tail surfaces are different for each type; and the longer P-63 fuselage puts the cockpit farther ahead of the wing than on the P-39. An identification feature when the landing gear is down is the straight-legged profile of the P-63 nose-wheel strut, instead of the castering crook for the nosewheel fork evident on the P-39. And the P-63 used a flat front windscreen of armor glass, straying from the P-39's use of a curved front windscreen with an internally-mounted flat armor glass panel. All of this adds up to a brand-new airplane design.

The characteristic cabin doors can be fitted to either aircraft. Although the basic part number for some P-63A doors begins with the prefix 15- (a Bell model number identifier for the P-39D), suffix numerals differ.[4] Other minor parts on P-63s appear to have P-39-derived numbers (the manual main gear extension handle, for example, begins

The NACA tested a P-63A with its own version of a tall tail which circumstantially looks like the F-model tail, but without dorsal or ventral fins added by Bell to the P-63F. (Peter M. Bowers collection)

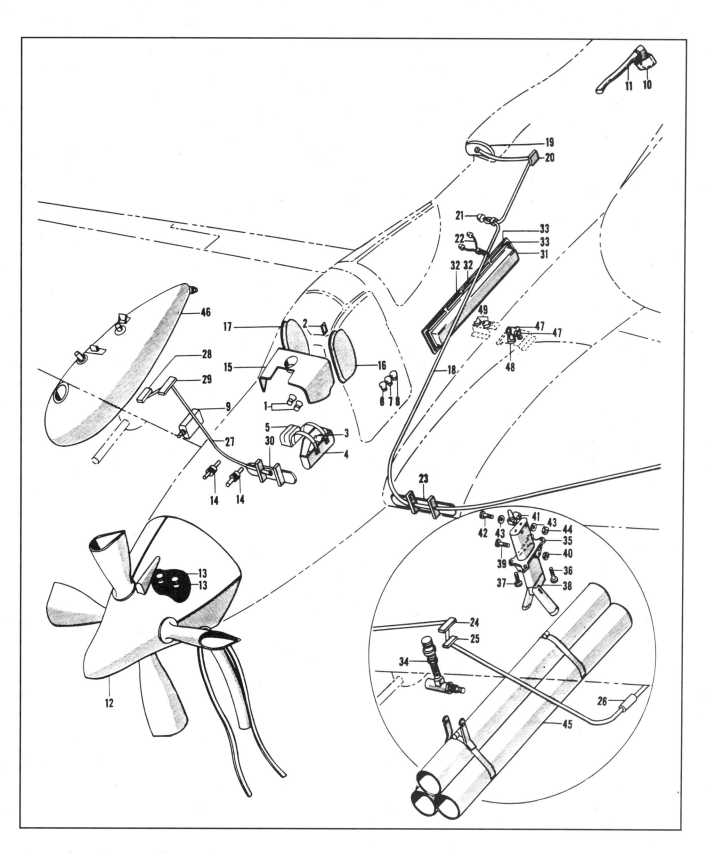

A page from the P-63E Illustrated Parts Book shows this model's ability to use three-tube MX-241 rocket launchers (part number 45) under the wings outboard of the machine gun. Parts 15, 16, and 17 are windshield anti-glare shields used in conjunction with an N-9 gunsight. A crash ax (part 11) was stowed in the aft fuselage where it could be reached by rescuers to help free a trapped pilot. Gun camera location (part number 9) was in the right wing. (USAFM)

P-63A shows characteristic exposed crescents of retracted mainwheels due to lack of inboard "flipper" doors. Even after many USAAF Kingcobras were delivered in natural metal finish like this example, P-63s for the Soviet Union were camouflaged olive drab and gray. (Bell photo via USAFM)

with the prefix 12-, dating back to the YP-39.)[5] But in the main, the two Bell fighters are not made from the same mold.

Production P-63As were already on order before the original XP-63 flew, and these began deliveries in October 1943.[6] The standard armament for P-63s was two nose-mounted and two wing gondola-mounted .50-caliber machine guns, plus a 37-MM cannon firing through the propeller hub. Beginning with deliveries of the P-63A-9BE and later versions, the M10 cannon replaced the M4 which had been standard since Airacobra production. With this change to the M10, the Kingcobra could carry 58 rounds of 37-MM ammunition instead of the M4's allotment of only 30 rounds.[7]

Where the P-39 Airacobra adhered to only a centerline shackle for a bomb or drop tank, Bell introduced a pair of underwing shackles on the Kingcobra beginning with the P-63A-6BE, while retaining the centerline shackle as well. The P-63A could carry a 75-gallon tank on each shackle, or the centerline could host a 175-gallon ferry tank. A USAAF tactical planning document showed use of the 175-gallon centerline tank only on A-models. The underwing shackles meant Kingcobras so equipped could carry as many as three 500-pound (or smaller) bombs.[8]

Late P-63As posted a high speed of 410 miles an hour at 25,000 feet, dropping to 402 miles an hour at 30,000 feet.[9] This approached the speeds of the P-51D Mustang, which clocked 437 miles an hour at 25,000 feet. Production of P-63As totaled 1,725 aircraft.[10] But while the Kingcobra was a delightful speedster to fly, its essential design rationale dated back to the P-39 era, where range was not emphasized. As with its Airacobra predecessor, the Kingcobra's mid-engine layout was not suited to fuselage fuel tankage.

Next production variant of the Kingcobra was the P-63C, with a mainwheel track narrower by four inches than that of A-models, and a war-emergency horsepower rating of 1,800 horsepower at sea level with water injection for its V-1710-117 engine. First accepted in

Six silver USAAF P-63As run up their Allisons in unison; USAAF Kingcobra operations, other than the highly-modified RP-63 Pinballs, were comparatively rare.

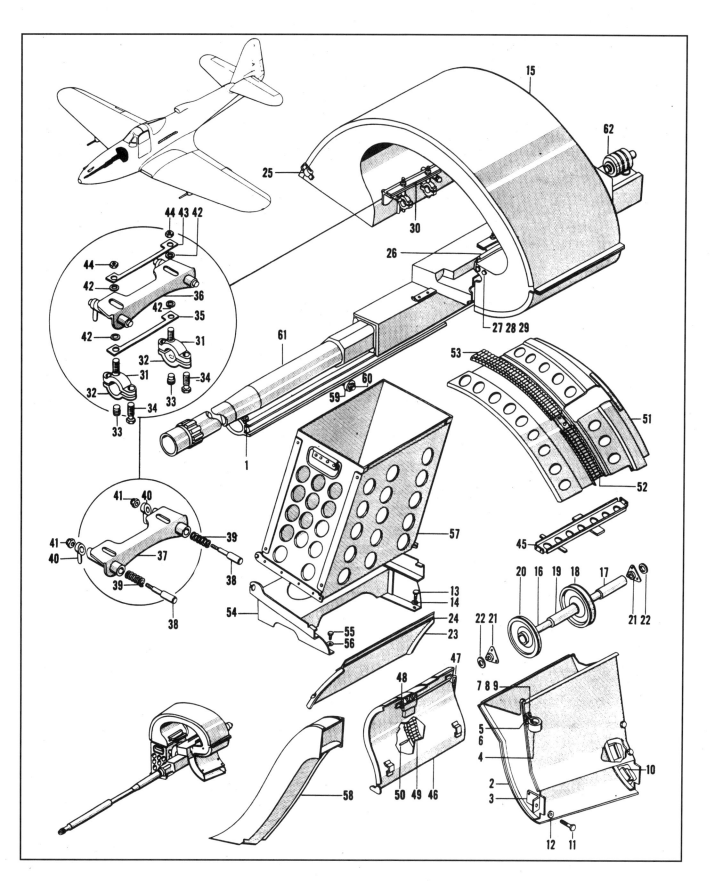

High-capacity M10 37-millimeter cannon was fitted to some P-63s, as depicted in this P-63E parts manual drawing. Ammo box (part 57) and chute (part 15) were improved over earlier M-4 cannon, giving greater capacity to the M10. (USAFM)

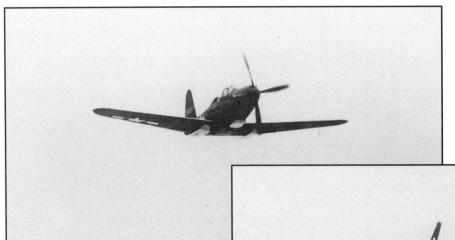

P-63A (42-68887) tested snow skis that retracted nearly flush with the wings and fuselage. Problems with excessive turn radius and other ground handling quirks were eventually largely overcome, but USAAF ski fighters remained in the test world. (USAFM)

December 1944, the C-model Kingcobra featured a ventral fin similar in appearance to the one Bell devised for some P-59 Airacomet jets. Three hundred P-63Cs were allotted to Free French forces, although it is likely only about two-thirds that number were actually received; some of these served the French Air Force well after World War Two ended.[11]

A slight increase in wingspan from 38 ft., 4 in., to 39 ft., 2 in., plus a bulbous sliding bubble canopy, heralded the lone P-63D, which was followed by 13 more conventional long-span P-63Es in flight testing by May 1945, too late to see production, although 2,930 E-models had been ordered and later cancelled.[12] The P-63E-1BE could be fitted with a pair of three-tube rocket launcher clusters, one under each wing, in addition to the standard armament of earlier Kingcobras.[13]

The last Kingcobra variant, the P-63F, powered by the V-1710-135, featured a noticeably taller vertical tail as well as the ventral fin. Two were built (USAAF serials 43-11719 and 43-11722).[14]

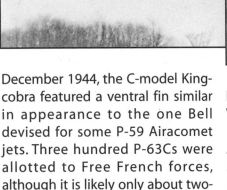

In the heat of a July day in 1944, mechanics worked on the brakes of a P-63 in a hangar at Ephrata Army Airfield in central Washington state. The lower main landing gear door has been removed to facilitate access; upper main gear door is still in place near oleo strut portion of upper gear leg. (Air Force Historical Research Agency)

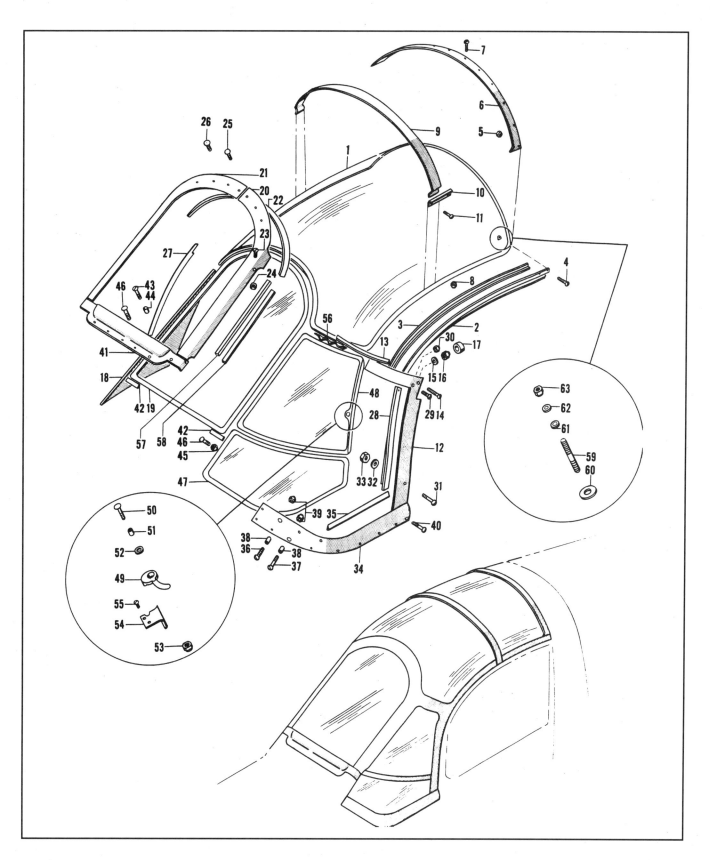

P-63E cockpit glazing drawing shows top Plexiglas panel to be one piece, with a retaining strip in the middle. This may explain photos showing some early P-39s with no center strip, since it did not divide two pieces of Plexiglas. Flat, curved-top armor glass front windscreen of P-63 was a simplification over earlier P-39 curved windscreen with interior armor glass.

1944, the USAAF tallied 339 P-63s on hand in the continental United States, the highest monthly total listed.[15]

Ski King

Between July 1943 and February 1945, design, development, and flight testing of skis on a P-63 involved the USAAF, Bell Aircraft, and Luscombe Engineering, makers of the skis. The testbed Kingcobra operated with skis at Lake Ouimet, Montreal, Canada, and at the Bell factory.[16]

Nearly 2,500 P-63s were delivered to the Soviet Union, where they performed credible service. The Kingcobra in USAAF hands was not destined for combat, although a number were shot at in one of World War Two's most unusual gunnery training schemes. P-63 production totaled 3,303 units — not bad for a fighter the U.S. did not take into battle (excepting the unorthodox shoot-down of a Japanese incendiary balloon by a Kingcobra in the western U.S. in March 1945).

By August 1945, the USAAF logged factory acceptances of 3,273 Kingcobras; only a few RP-63G manned target aircraft remained to be delivered. USAAF statistics show 31 Kingcobras being accepted in 1943, mushrooming to 1,786 in 1944 and 1,456 in 1945, even as P-39 production also occupied Bell's facilities into 1944. By the end of August

The first of two sets of skis attached to the P-63 used the same main skis as had been devised for the P-51. According to a USAAF test report: "The nose ski was designed quite similar to the P-38…" The P-63 nose ski did not swivel, and retracted flat up against the fuselage. The main skis, according to the report, "retracted flat up against the bottom of the wing. No fairing was used, since the curvature of the skis conformed closely to the bottom curvature of the wing section." As was experienced with a P-47 on skis, the first set of Kingcobra skis provided limited turning ability; due to engine torque, and prop-wash over the tail, only lefthand turns of large radius — about 300 feet — could be made on the frozen surface, "and they could only be made by using strong power and full rudder."[17]

P-63A shows 75-gallon underwing tanks plus centerline 175-gallon ferry tank. Four-blade Aeroproducts propeller has gray/silver blades. (USAFM)

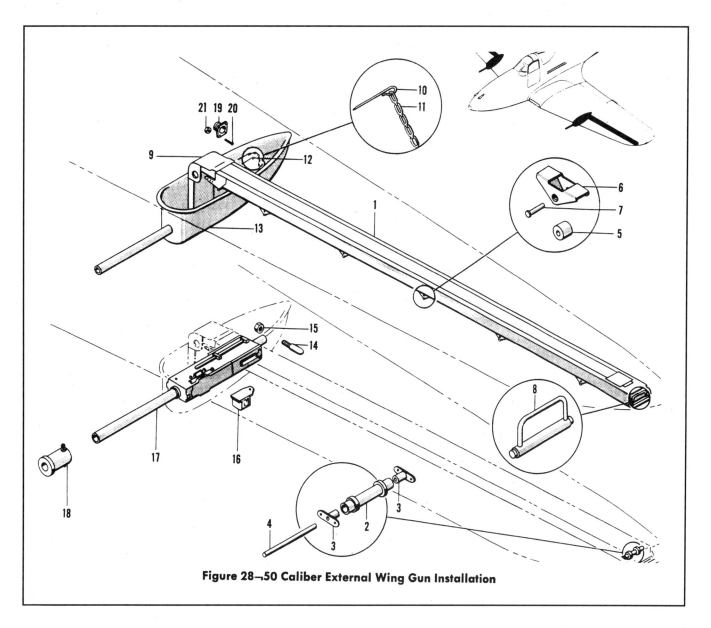

Figure 28–.50 Caliber External Wing Gun Installation

P-63E wing gun drawing shows long, thin ammunition box (part number 1) running outboard of the weapon. M-2 .50-caliber machine gun was mounted on its side in underwing pod.

The non-steering nose ski was subsequently reworked to allow it to slide sideways in an effort to enhance turning the ski-equipped Kingcobra. While some improvement was noted, turning to the right was still only achievable in excessively cumbersome maneuvers. While shallow snow appeared to offer no surprises during takeoff, the ski P-63 could be a handful in deep snow, according to the report: "Deep snow tests indicated that the nose ski was too heavily loaded. On takeoff it was impossible to hold the airplane in a straight path against the torque of the engine and a wide sweep to the left accompanied the ground run. After the speed picked up to a point where the nose ski could be lifted from the snow, takeoff was very rapid but before the elevator became effective, the acceleration was greatly retarded because the airplane seemed to be stubbing its toe due to the deep penetration of the nose ski."[18]

Improvising, the testers removed all runners from the bottom of the Kingcobra skis, save one 18-inch runner on the right main ski. According to the report, with this runner change: "Turns of fairly short radius could be made both to the left and to the right. The extra drag on the right ski approximately counteracted the engine torque and produced very good takeoff stability. However, it was found upon landing in deep snow that when the power was cut and

Not actually a P-63, this aircraft has been captioned as a P-39C. The curved windscreen and the design of the nosewheel strut indicate it is a P-39; evidently it was used as a testbed for a four-blade Curtiss Electric propeller, and for cooling inlets in the wing leading edge reminiscent of those used on P-63s. (Bell photo)

engine torque decreased, the drag on the right ski became excessive. This together with the high drag produced by the excessive nose ski penetration produced a quite severe groundloop, turning the airplane about 120 degrees."

An effort to gain the upper hand in controlling the ski-equipped P-63 on snow resulted in a second set of skis incorporating ski drag brakes engaged by the Kingcobra's brake pedals. But the testers were disappointed when "the master cylinder… had insufficient power to force enough area down under the ski to have a noticeable effect… Maneuverability was still quite limited and in most cases short radius turns required crew assistance on the wing tips." The second iteration of Kingcobra skis incorporated a redesigned nose ski with slightly more surface area and "considerably lower pitching axis. This alleviated the tendency for the nose ski to become buried in the snow and caused it to plane nicely out."[19]

Snowbound operations did not become a major combat feature in World War Two, and snow and ice

V-tail Kingcobra testbed, circa 1947, did not prove a convincing improvement over heavier conventional tail. (Bell via Peter M. Bowers)

Sweptwing P-63 hybrid became the Navy's L-39 used to test low-speed flying characteristics of swept wings, to give the Navy information useful for proposed jet fighters that would be expected to land at slow speeds on aircraft carriers.

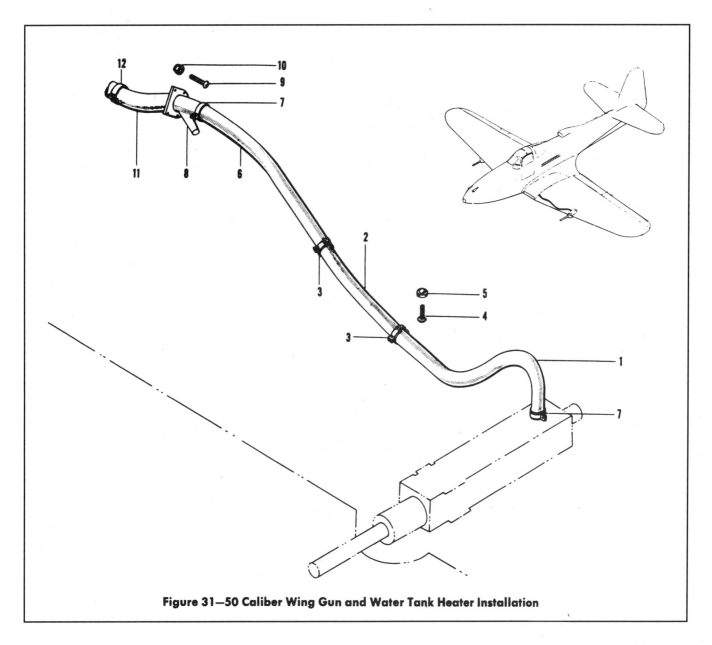

Figure 31—50 Caliber Wing Gun and Water Tank Heater Installation

P-63E parts manual depicts wing gun and water tank heater installation, using a hose to keep the machine gun warm enough to function at altitude. (USAFM)

tires served most scenarios encountered.

SWEPTWING KING

Bell Aircraft had a justly deserved reputation for entering into experimental programs. With surplus Kingcobras available in 1946, and engineers willing to explore new concepts, the U.S. Navy opted for two modified Kingcobras with which to study sweptwing phe-

nomena in the low end of the speed range. Using P-63A fuselages and P-63E wings attached with wedge-shaped inserts to produce sweepback of 35 degrees and no dihedral, a short-lived unofficial designation of P-63N gave way to formal Navy nomenclature of L-39 for the two test aircraft. The Navy Kingcobra sweptwing testbeds received Bureau of Aeronautics (BuAer) numbers 90061 and 90062.

Squared wingtips, parallel to the line of flight, were fabricated. While the nosewheel was retractable on the L-39s, the main gear, which could not retract outward with the wings swept without elaborate modifications, was fixed in the down position, with the main gear wells skinned over. Numerous configurations of leading edge slats were tried on the two L-39s, in an attempt to retain airflow over the swept wings at low speeds, to pro-

Seasoned Bell pilot Alvin "Tex" Johnston, more than four decades after the L-39 program, recalled: "I practiced for three days, trying to keep that dude off its back, and it was impossible."[20]

The best mix for leading edge devices was found to be between 40 and 60 percent of the leading edge span. But the utility of the L-39 did not end with this ascertainment; the second of the two L-39s was kept on hand by Bell to derive data for the sweptwing X-2 research rocket aircraft then in development.[21]

VEE '63

Other radical Kingcobra tests included the modification of a P-63A to use a V-tail, followed in 1948 with a small U.S. Air Force contract to Bell to modify an RP-63G with a slightly different V-tail. In both cases, some controllability problems emerged in low-speed regimes. Any advantages promised by the lighter weight and lower drag of a V-tail were offset by the handling quirks.

The Kingcobra has come to be viewed as fulfilling the promise of the original Airacobra, vindicating Bell and Allison. Its fortuitous arrival by late 1943 allowed the USAAF to retain and standardize on the P-51 for much of America's fighter needs, while providing Lend-Lease partners with a viable late-war combat aircraft, the P-63.

Bell's wartime fighter family posed for a company photograph with America's first jet aircraft, a P-59, closest to camera, followed by a P-63A (42-69417), a P-39Q (42-19597) and the experimental lightweight XP-77 interceptor. This P-39 eventually became the Confederate Air Force's example, painted in Soviet markings and later in USAAF olive and gray.

mote controllability of future sweptwing aircraft intended for aircraft carrier operations.

Even the testbeds needed testing to minimize undesirable traits not related to the intended test program. Four-foot fuselage plugs were inserted at the production break between the Kingcobra's main fuselage section and the tail section. In addition to placing the tail farther aft on these sweptwing oddities, the plug was designed to mount the tail with a reduction in angle of incidence. Enlarged ventral fins completed the look, and the L-39s were ready to test at low speeds approaching stalls.

With no slats, the L-39 stalled with little or no warning, rolling abruptly. With slats deployed over 100 percent of the leading edges of the wings, results were again unsatisfactorily marred by dangerous rolls.

[1] Howard Mingos, editor, *The Aircraft Yearbook for 1944*, Lanciar, New York, NY, 1944. [2] "Tactical Planning Characteristics and Peformance Chart", USAAF, 28 April 1945. [3] Birch Matthews, *Cobra! Bell Aircraft Corporation — 1934-1946*, Schiffer, Atglen, Pa., 1996. [4] USAAF Air Technical Service Command, *Interchangeability Cross Reference Charts*, T.O. No. 00-45S-1, October 1944. [5] *USAAF Parts Catalog for Airplanes — Army Model P-63E-1*, AN 01-110FP-4B, 5 August 1945. [6] Ray Wagner, *American Combat Planes*, Doubleday, Garden City, New York, 1968. [7] "Tactical Planning Characteristics and Peformance Chart", USAAF, 28 April 1945. [8] *Ibid*. [9] *Ibid*. [10] Ray Wagner, *American Combat Planes*, Doubleday, Garden City, New York, 1968. [11] *Ibid*. [12] *Ibid*. [13] "Tactical Planning Characteristics and Peformance Chart", USAAF, 28 April 1945. [14] Birch Matthews, *Cobra! Bell Aircraft Corporation — 1934-1946*, Schiffer, Atglen, Pa., 1996. [15] *Army Air Forces Statistical Digest — World War II* — Headquarters, USAAF, Office of Statistical Control, December 1945. [16] Report, *Fighter Ski Development Including P-36, P-40, P-38, P-51, P-47, and P-63*, by Capt Allen C. Carlson, Army Air Forces, Headquarters Air Technical Service Command, AAF Technical Report No. 5293, circa 1946. [17] *Ibid*. [18] *Ibid*. [19] *Ibid*. [20] From remarks made during a banquet presentation by A.M. "Tex" Johnston for the McChord Air Museum, Tacoma, Washington. [21] Birch Matthews, *Cobra! Bell Aircraft Corporation — 1934-1946*, Schiffer, Atglen, Pa., 1996.

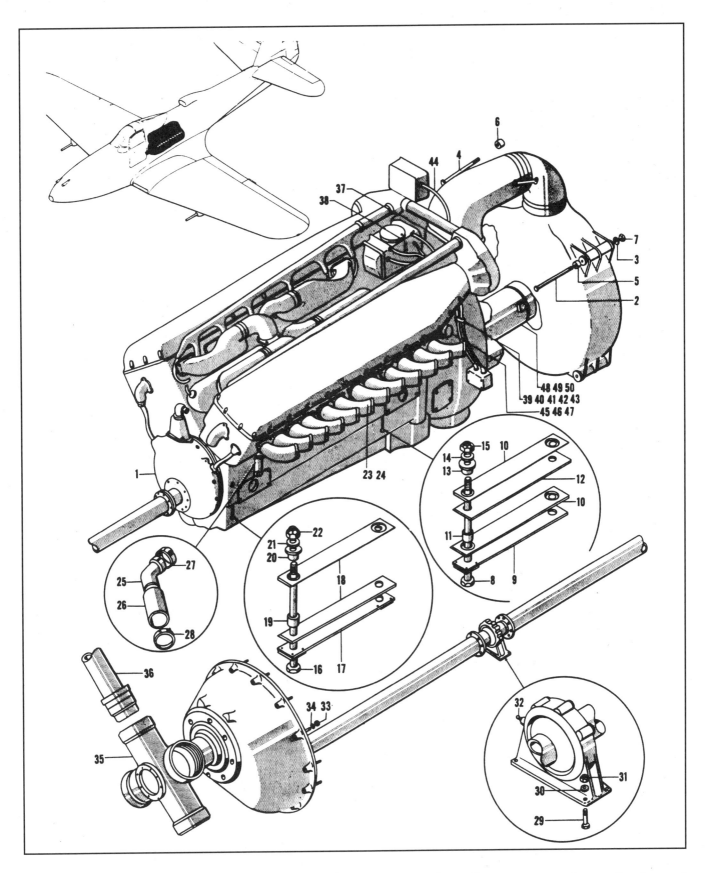

Powerplant drawing shows P-63E-model's beefy Allison V-1710-109 with auxiliary stage supercharger. Bearing and pillow block, detailed in circle at lower right of page, linked two sections of drive shaft, typical of P-39 and P-63 construction. Only 13 P-63Es were built by war's end. (USAFM)

EXPORT AIRACOBRAS

The Airacobra was tested and found wanting by the British Royal Air Force, even as the Soviet Union embraced the P-39 with gusto. As was the case with several American-made fighters and bombers, the Airacobra was earmarked for Allied use as well as U.S. service even before America entered the Second World War.

The Air Corps and the American aircraft industry in the late 1930s faced an unusual and sometimes strained period in their relationship. The Air Corps did not want to see finite U.S. production capability obligated to producing warplanes for foreign nations; further, Air Corps planners were loathe to sell America's most modern military technology overseas. Yet the Air Corps was unable to place large orders on its own behalf, and some companies like the fledgling Bell Aircraft Corporation were stretched thin on meager Air Corps funds. The U.S. tried encouraging American manufacturers to increase their physical plants to allow more aircraft to be built, but without orders on which to base such expansion, it was not likely to take place.[1]

Following the September 1939 German invasion of Poland by about two months, the U.S. Congress repealed an embargo on selling warplanes to belligerents; the time was right for the British and French governments to place orders for American warplanes.[2]

A French order for 165 Airacobras plus an equivalent 35 machines in spare parts was proposed to Bell on 19 April 1940 in a joint letter from the British and French Purchasing Commissions, which set down the specifics of Airacobra orders those countries desired. In the letter, the French and British representatives said: "We propose to purchase from you two hundred (200) (165 airplanes plus the dollar value of 35 airplanes in spare parts as specified by us) Bell Airacobra P-400 Pursuit Airplanes (P-39 Type) to be manufactured, sold, and delivered by you…"[3] [Author Birch Matthews

Looking full of promise, a line of 13 P-400s in full Royal Air Force regalia soon proved disappointing to the British; most of their export Airacobras went to the hard-pressed USAAF or the Soviet Union. Aircraft nearest camera, serial AH585, shows unusual six-stack exhaust configuration with flared exits. These 601 Squadron P-400s were photographed on the vast grassy field at Duxford. (Bowers collection)

The M4 37-mm cannon which equipped so many export Airacobras used an ovoid ammunition magazine that conformed to the cowl curvature, and separated in left and right pieces.

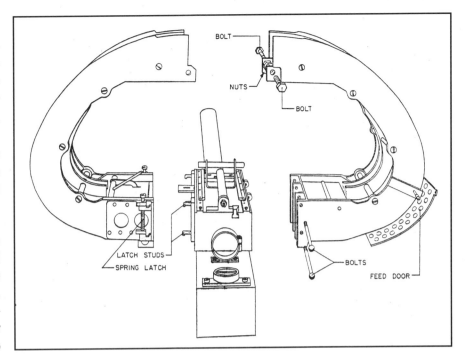

suggests "P-400" may have been coined by Bell Aircraft Corporation as a marketing term, hinting at a 400-mph pursuit airplane.]

The French proposal contained a proviso to pay for Air Corps-derived technology: "In addition to the price to be paid for said airplanes… we will pay a total of $360,000 representing the amount required by the United States Government to be paid by us with respect to development costs of the United States Army, it being agreed that payment of such amount will serve to effect the release to us of all future deliveries of this type of airplane manufactured by you insofar as such development costs are concerned without any further payment for any development costs."[4]

By the end of June 1940, France was overrun by Germany and French aircraft orders could not be filled. In evident anticipation of such a contingency, the April proposal to Bell included provision for "assignment of all or a part of such contract to the British Government

One of three Lend-Lease P-39Cs furnished to the RAF, this example appears to be fitted with a 20-mm cannon. (Bowers collection)

upon assumption of corresponding liabilities..."[5] On 24 June 1940, the British Purchasing Commission notified Bell Aircraft, "that on June 17, 1940, the French State assigned and transferred to this Government its interest in all existing contracts between you and the French State."[6]

After the initial French contract proposal, the number of finished Airacobras was raised to 170 aircraft, with the equivalent spares reduced to 30. Another agreement between the British and Bell, signed 10 July 1940, added "250 additional P-39 type airplanes" to the quantity being built for Great Britain. Bell agreed to accelerate its delivery schedule to get all 450 of the British aircraft and spares delivered by September 1941. To assure the Air Corps its P-39 orders would not languish in the backwash of the British purchase, Bell vice president and treasurer Ray Whitman wrote the Air Corps Materiel Division chief: "In connection with, and as part of this acceleration, we are advancing the deliveries of the last 60 P-39D airplanes from October and November, 1941 as originally scheduled, to January and February 1941 which means that the Air Corps will receive the last of the 93 P-39s now on order by February 1941." Whitman continued: "Also in this connection we are establishing a production rate of 90 airplanes per month

Multiple views of Airacobra I (P-400) AH573 show Bell factory camouflage that followed hard panel lines for demarcation between upper and lower surfaces. This Aircraft is fitted with 12 exhaust ports per side, common to P-400s. Wing guns have slotted cooling jackets visible. Top canopy retaining strip is not installed, revealing one-piece Plexiglas panel over pilot's head. (Bowers collection)

starting in May, 1941, 40 of which are U.S. Army Air Corps deliveries and the balance assigned to the British. It is emphasized that the new British order for 250 additional P-39 type airplanes will not delay the new and greatly-accelerated deliveries to the Air Corps."[7]

The Airacobra, designed to meet an Air Corps specification, became a financially-viable product for Bell more because of a 450-aircraft commitment from the British than due to early Air Corps production orders. However, Whitman acknowledged in his 15 July 1940 communication to the Air Corps Materiel Division chief: "We have just been advised, by special delivery letter from the Assistant Secretary of War, that we are now scheduled to receive orders from you for 120 additional P-39 airplanes plus a further order of 503 of this type which, according to the letter, are to be delivered by April 1, 1942."[8] Bell Aircraft was now squarely in the business of mass producing Airacobras for both the United States and its allies.

Unit price of the first French-ordered Airacobras was computed at $44,982, boxed for export at Buffalo, New York, and not counting the cost of items such as engine, drive shaft, gearbox, propeller, armament, and radio, which were to be furnished by the purchaser.[9] When the British added an additional 250 Airacobras to the order they assumed from the French, the unit

A P-400 was photographed during the crating process, for shipment to Great Britain. Airacobra shipping crates evolved as experience was gained in sending the little fighters overseas. (Musee de l'Air via Bowers collection)

A P-400 with a ferry tank came to grief in England in 1943, probably while being prepared for USAAF use in North Africa. To lift the crippled aircraft, a rod has been inserted in the lifting tube hole in the nose, with a rope slung beneath it. Long muzzle of 20-MM cannon is evident in propeller spinner. Straight edged camouflage demarcation on this aircraft does not follow panel lines as on earlier P-400s painted at the factory. (Air Force photo)

Converted to USAAF use, P-400 number BW114 was photographed in Australia in 1942 with its British serial and fin flash, and American stars. Overhead canopy retaining strip is installed on this aircraft. (Peter M. Bowers collection)

P-400s in USAAF service in the south Pacific sometimes adopted popular sharkmouth motif. Wing guns of this example have later-style cooling jackets perforated with circular holes instead of elongated slots. (Peter M. Bowers collection)

price slipped to $36,540, reflecting economies of mass production.

Bell Aircraft noted that the British could receive some of their Airacobras with larger diameter main tires than the standard 26-inch by 6-inch P-39 main tires: "It shall be possible to fit a 28-inch by 7-inch tire on the main wheels without other change to the airplane than removing the wheel fairing. Bell agrees to equip 125 airplanes with main wheel tires 26 inches by 6 inches, complete with fairings, and 125 airplanes with main wheel tires 28 inches by 7 inches, without wheel fairings, and to supply without additional cost 125 sets of main wheel tires 28 inches by 7 inches and 125 sets 26 inches by 6 inches. Performance guarantees apply only to airplanes equipped with 26-inch by 6-inch tires with wheel fairings."[10]

The P-400 used to verify Bell's performance figures for the British included several drag-reduction features. Posting a top true airspeed of 391 miles an hour, this P-400's performance could not be taken as routine for the lot, and no doubt contributed to subsequent British disappointment with their Airaco-

A crewman stands beside the characteristically-used right side door of a P-400 in the Pacific. Long Airacobra nosewheel struts frequently were painted dark green or olive. Propeller is black and yellow on this example. (Leo M. Myers collection)

Rare bird is this Royal Australian Air Force P-39F (ex-41-7119), RAAF number A53-1. This Airacobra appears to have an add-on baffle or deflector immediately in front of the armor plate bolted at the base of the front windscreen. (Peter M. Bowers collection)

bra I variants, as the P-400 was called in British service. (For a brief period, the RAF called the P-400 the Caribou before mercifully reverting to the name already in vogue in the United States for the P-39.)

AIRACOBRAS IN ENGLAND

Three P-39Cs made available to the British in July 1941 proved a letdown to the RAF pilots who flew them. Inferior in performance to the vaunted Spitfire Vb, especially at altitude, the low-level potential of the Airacobra was never fully exploited by the RAF. When the first P-400 Airacobra Is began arriving late that same month, earlier British experience with the sample P-39Cs was confirmed, with speed topping out at 355 miles an hour at 13,000 feet.[11]

RAF No. 601 City of London Squadron converted to Airacobras from Hawker Hurricanes in August 1941. While reveling in the admit-tedly-slower Airacobra's flight qualities, the pilots of 601 Squadron noted a number of other shortcomings, including erratic compass readings. (The use of a stamped steel instrument panel may have caused faulty compass readings in early Airacobras; later models of the P-39 used a remote-reading compass head in the panel instead of a magnetic compass.)

September 1941 saw four Airacobra Is placed on operational status at Manston in the UK, flying missions over the French coast on 9

French P-39N (42-9410) has muzzle tubes over wing guns as were applied to many Airacobras. (Allain Pelletier via Peter M. Bowers)

Red-starred P-39Q-5s on their way to the Soviet Union lined the ramp at Ladd Field, Alaska, parked near Soviet Lend-Lease A-20s and B-25s in July 1943. Some Soviet Airacobras were used without wing guns. (Air Force Museum via Peter M. Bowers)

and 11 September 1941, in spite of lingering problems with the compass. The City of London Squadron subsequently re-equipped with Spitfires early in 1942; the British shunted their Airacobra Is to the Soviets, and P-400s still in the United States after the Japanese bombing of Pearl Harbor were assimilated into the USAAF, some seeing combat in the south Pacific. A sprinkling of Airacobras saw testbed use in the United Kingdom, including arresting gear trials, with the last of the RAF Airacobras retiring in March 1948.[12]

SOVIET 'COBRAS

It has become oft-repeated lore of World War Two that the Airacobra, disdained by some American and British fliers, was welcomed and exploited by daring Soviet pilots. Researchers have credited Soviet leader Joseph Stalin with specifically coveting P-39s from his sometimes-uneasy American allies. Part of the Soviet gusto for P-39s stems from the nature of their war with Germany, where fighting was never far from tactical airfields.

French P-39Q (44-3172) carries a late-style stamped steel drop tank. (Allain Pelletier via Peter M. Bowers)

Soviet Airacobras were in evidence at a Russian airfield used by USAAF B-17s during a shuttle mission in 1944. Airacobra nearest camera does not have wing guns. Variances in red stars include the application of a star to the tail of only one of the P-39s in the photo. (Peter M. Bowers collection)

This did much to neutralize the Airacobra's range deficiencies. The Soviets also frequently flew their P-39s without wing guns, further lightening the aircraft to the benefit of performance. But the nose-mounted cannon was favored — if only it could carry more rounds.[13] This was rectified during P-63 Kingcobra production.

Ultimately, 4,924 Airacobras and 2,421 Kingcobras were earmarked for the Soviets. Delivery losses eroded these totals, and for P-39s and P-63s picked up by Soviet pilots in Alaska and flown across the Bering Sea, loss figures have not been tallied. It is reasonable to believe the Soviet Air Forces acquired a total of more than 7,000 Airacobras and Kingcobras.

Pilots of the Soviet Union frequently engaged German aircraft at medium-to-low altitudes, and Airacobra aces grew in the ranks of Soviet airmen.

B-24 historian Rhodes Arnold, who served in Alaska in 1945, chronicled a photo mission by Liberators of the 404th Bomb Squadron at war's end in mid-August 1945, to record bomb damage photos. Soviet forces had recently moved to Japanese areas in the cold North Pacific region. In a startling precursor of the as-yet unknown cold war, the USAAF Liberator crews were

A wartime German display of captured Allied aircraft included a dark-starred Soviet Airacobra near center of picture. This may be a former British Airacobra I (P-400). Even this captured example has the righthand door — the preferred entry — open. (Peter M. Bowers collection)

met by American-built P-63s with red star insignia, flown by Soviet pilots who, while not firing at the B-24s, tried unsuccessfully to thwart the photo mission by flying close to the Americans.[14]

In the post-Cold War era of information exchanging between elements of the former Soviet Union and researchers in the United States, information has come to light indicating the Soviet Air Force still had on duty P-63C Kingcobras in Siberia in 1952. These were scrambled on at least one occasion in an unsuccessful effort to intercept a probing U.S. Air Force aircraft[15]

OTHER USERS

By May 1943, Free French fliers helping the Allied cause in North Africa began obtaining second-hand P-39Ns, which they used largely for maritime patrols to pro-

An Italian P-39Q in flight carries a U.S. general-purpose bomb, probably a 500-pounder, on its centerline shackle. When Italy realigned with the Allies, Italian pilots used P-39s in the Mediterranean Theater to help drive the Germans out. (Garry Pape collection)

tect friendly shipping. The older N-model Airacobras were replaced with new P-39Qs, as the Free French carried the war into Italy and southern France. About 300 Kingcobras were earmarked for France, although the number received is probably more like two-thirds of that. When the French began flying P-63Cs in the summer of 1945, the European war was over; French Kingcobras did see combat in Indochina after World War Two, beginning in 1946 and lasting until early 1951.

Disillusionment with Germany prompted a quick turnaround for many Italians after Italy was invaded by the Allies in 1943. By the following year, the Italian Co-Belligerent Force was receiving used P-39Ns and P-39Qs, totaling nearly 150 Airacobras. The Italians used them to strike at German transportation targets in northern Italy, where the Germans remained even after Italy changed sides. Some Italian P-39s were kept on strength, for training, as late as 1951.[16]

The Royal Australian Air Force (RAAF) used about 15 P-39s received from 5th Air Force, with the first delivered in 1942, as the threat of Japanese attacks upon Australia seemed plausible. They were returned to the USAAF by late 1943.

In the late 1940s, five P-63Es were delivered to the Honduran Air Force. This proved beneficial to some of these Kingcobras, prolonging their existence until they attracted notice as candidates for the civil warbird market years later.

At least one P-39 was reported to have fallen into German hands on the eastern front in mid-1943. It may have received a German aircraft code, indicating it may have been flown for some purpose — probably evaluation — by the Luftwaffe.[17]

A secondhand Italian P-39N shows evidence of its former USAAF heritage in the bars to either side of the Italian roundel on the fuselage. Aircraft probably was transferred from a 15th Air Force depot.

[1] Birch Matthews, Cobra! — *Bell Aircraft Corporation, 1934-1946,* Schiffer, Atglen, Pennsylvania, 1996. [2] *Ibid.* [3] Letter, British Purchasing Commission and French Purchasing Commission, to Bell Aircraft Corp. (Lawrence D. Bell, President), Subject: Proposal to buy 200 Airacobras, 19 April 1940. [4] *Ibid.* [5] *Ibid.* [6] Letter, British Purchasing Commission to Bell Aircraft Corp., Subject: Transfer of French contract to British, 24 June 1940. [7] Letter, Bell Aircraft Corp. (Ray Whitman, VP and Treasurer), to Chief, Materiel Division, U.S. Army Air Corps, Subject: Transmission of Anglo-French contracts for P-39 type airplanes, 15 July 1940. [8] *Ibid.* [9] Letter, British Purchasing Commission and French Purchasing Commission, to Bell Aircraft Corp. (Lawrence D. Bell, President), Subject: Proposal to buy 200 Airacobras, 19 April 1940. [10] Exhibit A, Addendum to Letter of July 9th, 1940, Bell Aircraft Corp., 9 July 1940. [11] A. J. Pelletier, *Bell Aircraft Since 1935,* Naval Institute Press, Annapolis, Maryland, 1992. [12] *Ibid.* [13] Birch Matthews, *Cobra! — Bell Aircraft Corporation, 1934-1946,* Schiffer, Atglen, Pennsylvania, 1996. [14] Rhodes Arnold, *The B-24/PB4Y in Combat — The World's Greatest Bomber,* Pima Paisano Publications, Reserve, New Mexico. [15] Conversation between the author and Ray Wagner, San Diego Aersospace Museum librarian, 19 January 1998. [16] Birch Matthews, *Cobra! — Bell Aircraft Corporation, 1934-1946,* Schiffer, Atglen, Pennsylvania, 1996. [17] Hans-Heiri Stapfer, *Strangers in a Strange Land,* Squadron/Signal, Carrollton, Texas, 1988.

'COBRAS IN COMBAT

After America's abrupt entry into World War Two through the pall of smoke at Pearl Harbor, Airacobras were pressed into combat service, logging missions with Fifth Air Force out of Port Moresby by April 1942. After decades of books and articles demeaning P-39s as dogfighters, a memo from Gen. Douglas MacArthur to Air Force chief Gen. Henry H. Arnold, dated 14 May 1942, bears notice. It contains a brief compendium of AAF pilot reports of engagements with Japanese fighters (listed as "0", for Zero). MacArthur's memo says: "In combat with '0' it is the opinion from different pilots that [the] P-39 is from 5 to 10 percent superior over [the] P-40." (Later, as altitude became an issue, P-40s were sometimes favored.) The memo conceded that the Zero had better climb and maneuverability than the P-39, but at low altitudes, "the P-39 is slightly faster at 325 miles per hour speed. P-39 can out-dive '0'..." The memo does call for fighters with higher altitude capabilities than those of either the P-39 or P-40 to be sent to the Pacific.[1]

United States Army Air Forces combat use of P-39s would dwindle by 1944, but the Soviet Union, a reoriented Italy, and France kept the Airacobra in battle through the end of the war in 1945. USAAF P-39s showed up in Alaska, the Mediterranean, and the South and Central Pacific, where late N- and Q-models achieved their zenith in the USAAF as destroyers of Japanese shipping and transport.

Meanwhile, the P-39 gave many AAF pilots in the United States their first taste of a single-seat, high-per-

Clean P-39D-1 (41-28313) trained fighter pilots stateside. This aircraft has faint evidence of medium green camouflage blotching on the leading edge of the vertical fin, prescribed for many USAAF warplanes to break up the straight lines made by the wings and tail. Star insignia has red surround used briefly between June and August 1943, although examples of this style probably lingered. Worthy of note when studying Airacobra paint and markings in service is the color of the propeller. Here, it is painted black with yellow tips; other photos in this volume depict P-39s with bare metal gray/silver blades.

On several wartime occasions, USAAF fighters were taken close to the fighting by U.S. navy aircraft carriers, from which the Army fighters launched, recovering on land. In 1944, 72nd Fighter Squadron Airacobras were rigged with disposable slings to allow them to be catapulted over the Pacific. (Air Force Historical Research Agency)

formance warplane. Some, like the determined young Chuck Yeager in training at Tonopah Army Airfield in Nevada, liked the curvy little fighter with the big gun. Yeager was a firm believer that practice makes perfect, and he maximized his training time in the P-39, paying attention to its quirks even as some of his fellow fliers rode spinning Airacobras to their deaths in the gritty high desert around Tonopah.

Some stateside bases kept Airacobras on hand to bounce bombers, giving student gunners a taste of real fighter tactics.

A comprehensive listing of all USAAF P-39 units is elusive; some fighter squadrons had Airacobras only briefly in training before switching to Mustangs or Thunderbolts for combat, while others wore out P-39s in grueling day-in, day-out sorties against a seemingly endless stream of Japanese barges bearing the stuff of war. A tally of P-39 units in the USAAF includes:[2]

8th Fighter Group — After some peacetime training with aircraft including P-39s, this group took

A 72nd Fighter Squadron P-39Q, flaps partially lowered to increase lift, hurtles past the forward edge of the carrier flight deck in 1944. Catapult sling is visible ahead of main landing gear. Apparent "bend" in landing gear is a phenomenon of curtain-style shutter in camera. (Air Force Historical Research Agency)

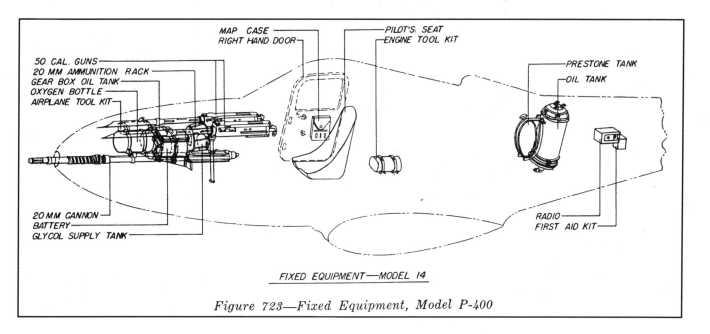

Figure 723—Fixed Equipment, Model P-400

Phantom view of a P-400 fuselage shows positions of .50 caliber nose guns and 20-MM cannon, surrounding an oxygen bottle located just ahead of the cannon drum magazine. P-400 airplane tool kit mounted to slope of forward fuselage beam.

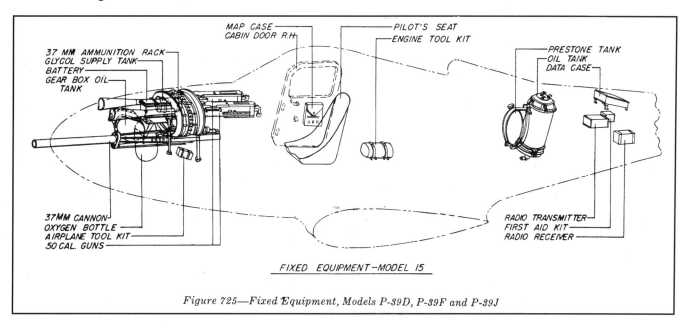

Figure 725—Fixed Equipment, Models P-39D, P-39F and P-39J

P-39Ds, Fs, and Js were depicted in a phantom view from Airacobra Erection and Maintenance manual that showed the 37-MM cannon ammunition magazine encircling the nose .50-caliber guns. Large blast tube funnels for 50-caliber guns installed on many P-39s were stainless steel, and protruded above the nose contour. Radio gear in aft fuselage was accessed through hinging doors in fuselage sides.

Airacobras to Australia and New Guinea in 1942 to fight under 5th Air Force; ultimately switched to P-38s.

15th Fighter Group — Included P-39s in its force for defense of the Hawaiian Islands circa 1941-42; received P-51s late in 1944.

16th Fighter Group — Had some P-39s in its complement before World War Two in the Canal Zone; converted to P-40s in 1941.

18th Fighter Group — Moved from Hawaii to the South Pacific in March 1943, and included P-39s in

A deck handler watches as a 72nd Fighter Squadron P-39 discards its catapult sling over the edge of the ship as the Airacobra charges into the air. (AFHRA)

its mixed roster of aircraft. Flew under 13th Air Force, and converted to P-38s by 1944.

20th Fighter Group — Flew P-39s and P-40s stateside during early World War Two as an air defense unit; converted to P-38s in January 1943 and went to England in August of that year.

21st Fighter Group — Activated in Hawaii on 21 April 1944, as part of 7th Air Force's defenses of those islands; first flew P-39s, later converting to P-38s and then P-51s before moving to Iwo Jima in early 1945.

26th Reconnaissance Group — P-39s were among its varied aircraft used to support the stateside training of ground forces before the unit was disbanded on 11 November 1943.

28th Bomb Group — P-39s were among the mixed bag of fighters and bombers flown by this unit between 1941 and 1943 in Alaska before specializing in B-24s and B-25s during 1944-45. Having trained for arctic warfare in 1941, the 28th Bomb Group formed part of Alaska's air defenses.

31st Fighter Group — Activated in February 1940, the 31st was an early user of P-39s in stateside maneuvers; sent to England in the summer of 1942 to fly Spitfires with 8th Air Force.

32nd Fighter Group — This group included P-39s on its flightline as

Bathing beauty adorned the right door of a 110th Tactical Reconnaissance Squadron P-39 in New Guinea, circa 1944. Pilot has a jungle camouflaged flightsuit beneath his yellow mae west life preserver. Legend on side of cockpit reads: "Pilot - Lt. J.T. Evans; Crew Chief - S/Sgt. Raver".

P-39s in sand bag revetments on Iceland, 2nd Air Base Group, 30 March 1942; example at left has barely-visible portion of red center to fuselage star, which was deleted that year to create a blue-and-white insignia. Airacobras ranging from Iceland occasionally had opportunities to chase German FW-200 Kondor four-engine maritime reconnaissance bombers. (Air Force photo)

part of the defense force for the Panama Canal; the unit was disbanded in November 1943.

33rd Fighter Group — The 33rd, activated on 15 January 1941 at Mitchel Field, New York, began training with P-39s but changed to P-40s not long after. Subsequently flew P-40s in North African combat beginning in 1942, and P-38s and P-47s in the China-Burma-India Theater in 1944-45.

35th Fighter Group — Trained with P-39s, as well as P-35s, P-36s, and P-40s following the group's activation on 1 February 1940. Moved to Australia and trained for combat in P-39s as part of 5th Air Force in 1942, flying from Australia and New Guinea.

36th Fighter Group — Moved to Puerto Rico in January 1941, and operated P-39s as well as P-40s as part of the Caribbean and Panama Canal defenses. Returned to the United States in the summer of 1943, subsequently equipping with P-47s and moving to England for combat.

48th Fighter Group — As the 48th Bombardment Group (Light) and later the 48th Bombardment Group (Dive), and then the 48th Fighter-Bomber Group, this unit, which served as a replacement training group, and furnished planes for maneuvers and some coastal patrols, included some P-39s in its mixed bag of warplanes at times between 1942 and 1944. It had already converted to P-47s and moved overseas before being redesignated as a fighter group in May 1944.

52nd Fighter Group — Trained and flew maneuvers in P-39s and P-40s in the U.S. in 1941-42 before moving to England in the summer of 1942 to fly Spitfires in the 8th AF.

53rd Fighter Group — Moved to the Panama Canal Zone in December 1941 and equipped with P-39s in defense of the Canal. Returned to the United States in November 1942 and served 3rd Air Force as a training unit with P-39s and other fighters.

54th Fighter Group — Flew P-39s in Alaska against Japanese forces in the Aleutians during the summer of 1942, earning a Distinguished Unit Citation. Later became a stateside P-51 replacement training unit.

Tattered snapshot of the 110th TRS P-39 seen in a previous photo, this view reveals the individual aircraft number on the nose to be 30. Shiny rows of rivets diverging beneath nose numbers suggest field repairs to longitudinal beam.

56th Fighter Group — Activated early in 1941 as the 56th Pursuit Group, this unit trained with P-39s and P-40s while serving as an air defense organization and operational training outfit; in the summer of 1942 it converted to P-47s and prepared for combat in Europe.

58th Fighter Group — As a stateside training unit, P-39s were among the fighters used to train replacement pilots in 1942 and into 1943. Later, this unit flew Pacific combat in P-47s.

59th Fighter Group — This stateside unit, designated the 59th Reconnaissance Group in April 1943 and the 59th Fighter Group that August, used P-39s to train pilots, with part of the group switching to P-40s about a month

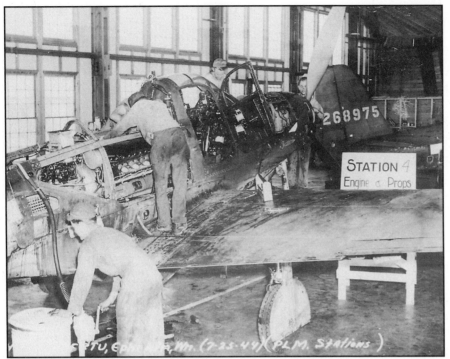

Servicing a well-worn P-39 at Ephrata, Washington, was messy business for five mechanics detailed to this Airacobra on 25 July 1944. With cowlings removed, the square intake of the carburetor can be seen behind a fuselage former to the left of the worker on the wing. In the background is one of Ephrata Army Airfield's Kingcobras. (Air Force photo)

before the unit was disbanded on 1 May 1944.

66th Reconnaissance Group — Based around the southeastern United States, this unit helped ground forces learn to work with airpower for reconnaissance and artillery spotting until its disbanding in April 1944. P-39s were part of the unit's complement at some time during its three-year wartime existence.

68th Reconnaissance Group — Included P-39s in its arsenal at some time; operated with 12th AF following patrols in the Gulf of Mexico and along the Mexican border after the attack on Pearl Harbor; disbanded on 15 June 1944.

69th Reconnaissance Group — Had some P-39s in its diverse inventory while stateside.

70th Reconnaissance Group — Flying primarily from west coast fields in the U.S., including Redmond and Corvallis, Oregon, and supporting ground units by providing appropriate air assets, the 70th flew some P-39s. The unit was disbanded on 30 November 1943. *(text continued on page 70)*

The 71st Tactical Reconnaissance Group at Dobodura solved some of its urgent supply needs by cutting a hatch in a wide ferry tank and making a cargo pod for P-39s capable of carrying items including tires, wheels, a manual air pump, and small boxes. (Via San Diego Aerospace Museum)

(Opposite page) Beginning with P-39Ks and later, the "basket" armor plate for the gearbox in the nose was replaced with flat plates that still provided head-on protection. The P-400 used a smaller piece of forward armor glass than subsequent P-39s used. On P-400s, this forward armor glass was peaked at the top; on the others, it had a gently arched top edge. P-400s were designed with armor plate to protect oxygen bottles in the nose.

THE COLOR OF 'COBRAS

The YP-39s, coalescing the general configuration of Airacobras to come, were introduced with natural metal finishes in 1940; at least some of the 13 YP-39s were painted "Dark Olive Drab" and "Neutral Gray", according to a Bell P-39/63 characteristics chart. The very similar P-39Cs carried standard Dark Olive and Neutral Gray coloring.[1] For latter-day restorations and modeling, the old Dark Olive Drab has been compared to the current Federal Standard color FS 34087; Neutral Gray is close to FS 36173.[2]

P-400s were painted Dark Earth and Green on upper surfaces and Sky Type S Gray on lower surfaces. P-39Ds were Dark Olive Drab and Neutral Gray; P-39D-1s and D-2s had Dark Olive Drab upper surfaces and Sky Type S Gray undersurfaces. The balance of P-39 production was Dark Olive and Neutral Gray.[3] During 1944, as P-39s were being overhauled at McChord Field in Washington, 4th Air Force decreed paint was to be stripped and Airacobras refurbished in natural

metal. While some Airacobras operated stateside in natural finish, the labor involved in stripping P-39s prompted McChord Field officials to get relief from this dictate. Bell correspondence from the field indicates some P-39s intended for use in the Mediterranean Theater of Operations received variegated camouflage similar to the P-400s (or possibly Dark Earth and Dark Olive Drab, according to USAAF markings research specialist Dana Bell).

The second RP-63A (42-69654), resplendent in orange—often used for its high-visibility when viewed from the same altitude—carried the defining nickname Pin Ball, with the smaller legend, Do Not Tilt, beneath the name. Top canopy section appears to be armored metal in the photo; other Pinballs used armor glazing there.
(Bell Textron via Dana Bell)

P-39 aft canopy and deck removed as a unit to facilitate servicing V-1710 engine, as mechanics in the Aleutian Islands were photographed doing. Ribbed metal .50-caliber ammo box is visible behind removed canopy deck section on ground in front of the aircraft.
(National Archives)

P-63As originally were specified to be Dark Olive Drab and Neutral Gray. Photos of camouflaged P-63Cs suggest the change from Neutral Gray to the even darker Sea Gray that was adopted for USAAF aircraft may have occurred. (The current Federal Standard equivalent for Sea Gray is FS 36118.) Photos show Soviet Kingcobras being delivered in olive and gray after USAAF P-63As and C-models were photographed in natural metal finish, probably indicating a continuing Soviet preference for camouflage not needed on stateside USAAF Kingcobras.

Inside the cockpit of a typical P-39, the interior door panels and other visible structure was painted flat dark green. Comparison of surviving original surplus P-39 cockpit furnishings suggests current Federal Standard FS 34096 is a good match for Airacobra cockpit interior green. The color of the interior of a later P-63 door appears more like FS 34097, one shade "greener". (Of course, these subjective comparisons were made more than a half-century after the parts were painted; the topic of accurate aircraft color is always subject to interpretation about fading, weathering and other factors.) Electrical switch boxes and the instrument panel in the Airacobra cockpit were dull black.

[1] "Aircraft Equipment Chart" for P-39 models, produced as a maintenance aid by Bell Aircraft Corp. during World War Two. [2] For more on USAAF colors, see Dana Bell's *Air Force Colors (Volumes 1 and 2)*, Squadron/Signal Publications, Carrollton, Texas. [3] "Aircraft Equipment Chart" for P-39 models, produced as a maintenance aid by Bell Aircraft Corp. during World War Two.

P-39Q (42-20740) used as a stateside trainer received a new engine, being run in as this Kodachrome was snapped during the war. Ground running of a P-39 Allison was tricky; the engine cooling system was prone to overheating. This perspective emphasizes the bullet-nosed streamlining favored by Bell, and later endorsed by a conscious copying of a .50-caliber bullet for the silhouette of the supersonic Bell X-1. (Richard Gambill collection via Merle Olmsted)

In a sporty civilian paint scheme popular in an era before warbirds had a life of their own, P-39Q N40A, a former two-seater, was an airport curiosity in California in 1959. Still evident in the photo are the dorsal and ventral fins applied to two-seat conversions during the war. After subsequent modifications by Mira Slovak, who flew N40A as Mr. Mennen, this Q-model was sold to the Confederate Air Force. (Photo by Milo Peltzer)

WARBIRD**TECH**
SERIES

Bright red Tipsy Miss *Kingcobra* was a late P-63C (44-4393, N62822) flown at the 1975 Reno air races by John Sandberg. Subsequently sold to an owner in Europe, this P-63 was destroyed in a fatal mishap in 1990. Racing modifications included clipped wingtips and large trailing edge wing/fuselage fillets, not visible in this photo. (Frederick A. Johnsen)

In the 1970s, the Confederate Air Force cornered the market on flyable P-39s. One of their two Airacobras was N6968 (42-19597), flown for many years in a Soviet-style green paint scheme, as photographed over Harlingen, Texas, during the October 1976 air show. (Photo by Frederick A. Johnsen)

For several years in the late 1970s, the Confederate Air Force flew P-39Q N40A in early P-400-style markings; previous owner Mira Slovak replaced a custom made wrap-around windscreen with flat-fronted structure from a P-63. N40A subsequently was sold to the Kalamazoo Air Museum in Michigan. (Photo by Frederick A. Johnsen)

Incorporating lessons learned on the XP-39, this gleaming silver pre-war YP-39 shows the general airframe traits of all production Airacobras to follow. Solid spinner indicates nose cannon is not installed; four cowling guns subsequently gave way to two, and guns were added in the wings later. (Peter M. Bowers collection)

Zebra-striped P-39s like this example awaiting its fate in a boneyard at Sandia, New Mexico, in 1946, once served as fighter targets for gunnery students with gun cameras before the advent of armored Kingcobras and frangible bullets made live-firing at target RP-63s a reality. (Don Alberts collection)

In the last half of the 1960s, an RP-63 Pinball, in spurious markings, was on display at the Fresno, California, airport. Highlights and shadows in the photo reveal aspects of Pinball armor, including steel baffles over the exhaust stacks. (Photo by Milo Peltzer)

WARBIRD**TECH**
S E R I E S

ITEM NO.	BELL DR. NO.	ARMOR PLATE AND GLASS DESCRIPTION	Weight	P-400	P-39 D	P-39 F	P-39 D-1	P-39 D-2	P-39 K-1	P-39 L-1	P-39 M-1	P-39 N-0	P-39 N-1	P-39 Q-1
1	14-855-001	Gear Box Armor Plate—5/8" Homogenous Steel Plate	95.45	X			X	X						
2	12-855-001	Gear Box Armor Plate—5/8" Homogenous Steel Plate	96.03		X	X								
3	26-855-001	Gear Box Armor Plate—5/8" Homogenous Steel Plate	70.74						X	X	X	X	X	X
4	14-855-011	Forward Oxygen Bottle Armor Plate—5/8" Homogenous Steel Plate	35.01	X										
5	14-855-044	Aft Oxygen Bottle Armor Plate—5/8" Homogenous Steel Plate	27.60	X										
6	14-855-004	Cabin Armor Plate 9/32" Homogenous Steel Plate	11.20	X										
6	14-855-004-12	Cabin Armor Plate 9/32" Homogenous Steel Plate	10.91				X	X	X	X	X	X	X	X
6	14-855-004-13	Cabin Armor Plate 9/32" Homogenous Steel Plate	11.20		AC 40-2991 TO AC 41-6781									
6	14-855-004-14	Cabin Armor Plate 9/32" Homogenous Steel Plate	11.20		AC 41-6782 TO AC 41-7344									
7	14-855-005	Forward Armor Glass—1½" Bullet Proof Glass	15.66	X										
8	15-855-020	Forward Armor Glass—1½" Armor Glass	21.72		X	X	X	X	X	X	X	X	X	X
9	14-855-002-2	Fumetight Bulkhead Armor Plate—9/32" Homogenous Steel Plate	14.51	X										
9	14-855-002-9	Fumetight Bulkhead Armor Plate—1/4" Face Hardened Plate	14.51				X	X						
10	15-855-002	Fumetight Bulkhead Armor Plate—5/8" Face Hardened Plate	27.00		X	X			X	X	X	X	X	X
11	14-855-008	Turnover Bulkhead Armor Plate—9/32" Homogenous Steel Plate	19.12	X										
12	15-855-008	Turnover Bulkhead Armor Plate—1/4" Face Hardened Plate	14.90		X	X	X	X	X	X	X	X	X	X
13	14-855-055	Aft Armor Glass—2½" Bullet Proof Glass	43.94	X	X	X								
14	14-855-070	Aft Armor Glass—2½" Bullet Proof Glass	44.17				X	X	X	X	X	X	X	X
15	15-855-019	Body Turnover Armor Plate—1/4" Face Hardened Plate	12.81		X	X	X	X	X	X	X	X	X	X
16	14-855-072-1	Main Oil Tank Armor Plate—6mm Homogenous Steel Plate	28.79	X										
16	14-855-072-2	Main Oil Tank Armor Plate—1/4" Face Hardened Plate	28.79		X	X	X	X	X	X	X	X	X	X

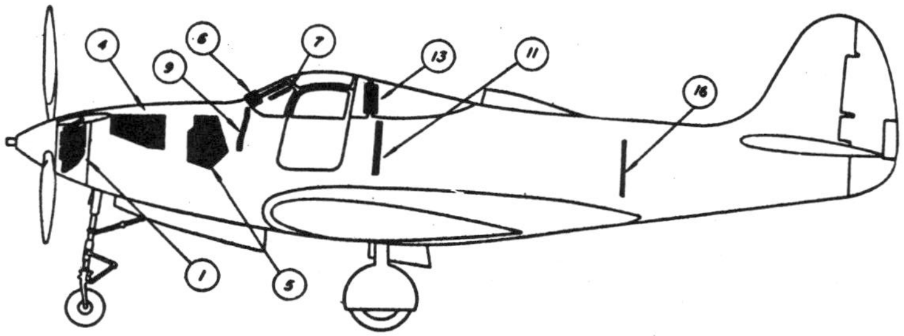

Figure 946—Armor Plate—Model P-400

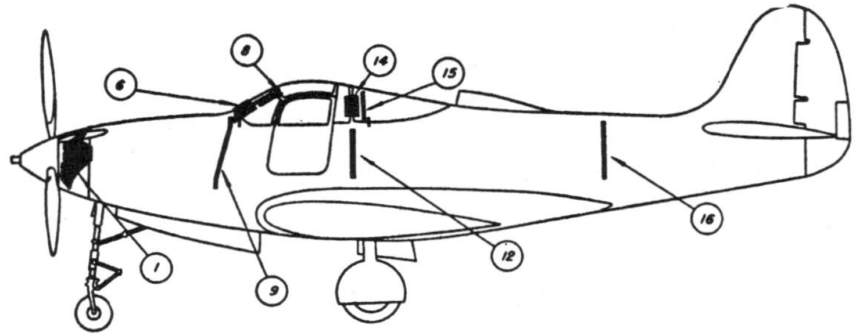

Figure 947—Armor Plate—Models P-39D-1 and P-39D-2

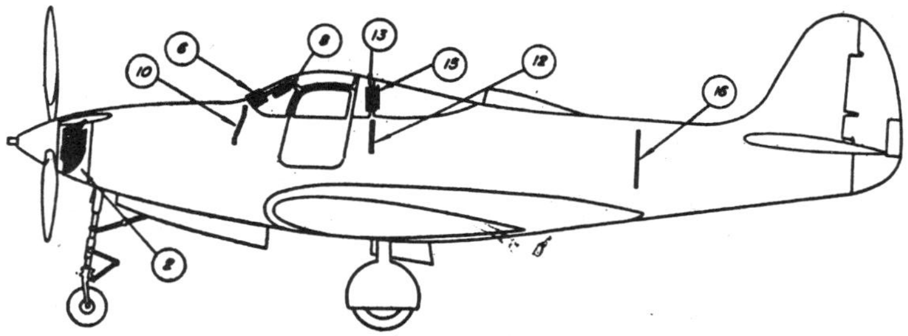

Figure 948—Armor Plate—Models P-39D and P-39F

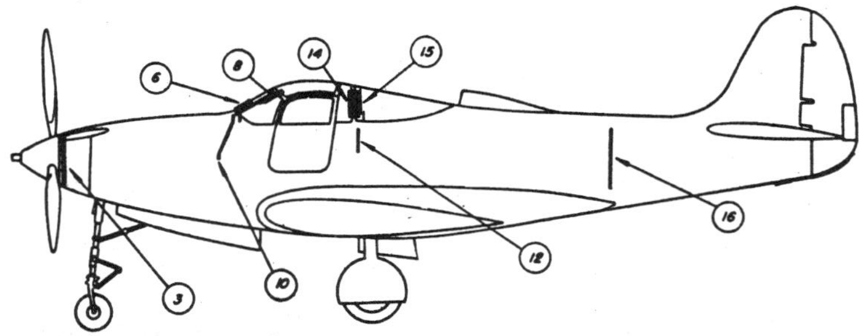

Figure 949—Armor Plate—Models P-39K-1, P-39L-1, P-39M-1, P-39N-O, P-39N-1 and P-39Q-1

TABLE OF ARMOR PLATE INSTALLATIONS

Rounded hole in the radio bay hatch of a 71st Tactical Reconnaissance Group P-39Q-5 (42-19975) was a reconnaissance camera installation. With camera modifications, this Airacobra probably was redesignated a P-39Q-6. Of note is unbordered national insignia on fuselage. (SDAM)

(text continued from page 64)
71st Reconnaissance Group — Activated in October 1941, this unit began training with P-39s and other aircraft. Moved to New Guinea under 5th Air Force, the 71st was known as the 71st Tactical Reconnaissance Group between May 1944 and May 1945. Into 1944, this group used P-39s extensively for armed reconnaissance, bombing and strafing Japanese targets. For May 1944, the Group historian wrote: "With our P-39s getting old enough to be 'combat happy', their pilots were finding need of more eyes — one to watch the plane, one to shoot with, one to gain enemy information, and one to use in avoiding ack-ack."[3] A number of P-39s brought back to the United States for restoration have been 71st Tactical Reconnaissance Group combat veterans.

Aircraft 24 and 25 of the 71st Tactical Reconnaissance Group in New Guinea have theater identification markings applied, including white wing leading edges and white tail section. These two P-39s had white tail paint applied over their serial numbers, making accurate identification of specific aircraft difficult, as there may have been more than one Airacobra assigned the same two-digit aircraft number on the nose, replacing a lost P-39 with the same identification number. (USAFM and Furler collections)

A 71st Tactical Reconnaissance Group P-39, nicknamed Classy Chassis above the nude painted on the door, carried individual aircraft identification number 20. The P-39N in the background has its serial number re-applied in a dark color over the white Allied recognition markings on the tail. In the shadows beneath its fuselage, Classy Chassis carries a general-purpose bomb on its centerline shackle. The 71st Tactical Reconnaissance Group elevated P-39 ground attack sorties to their zenith in the south Pacific in 1943-44.

72nd Reconnaissance Group — Used a variety of aircraft, including P-39s, on a variety of missions in the Panama Canal Zone circa 1942-43.[4]

74th Reconnaissance Group — This organization included P-39s at some time during its tenure as a stateside training unit working with ground forces.

75th Reconnaissance Group — Included P-39s in its stateside training role.

While preparing to depart England for North Africa, this P-39M made a mud-spattered belly landing in February 1943 Cockpit door has been removed and leaned by the nose; a safety-wired red handle inside cabin could be pulled to quickly release the door. Fuselage insignia of this Airacobra has yellow border applied to many aircraft sent to North Africa. (USAFM)

76th Reconnaissance Group — P-39s were listed as part of its inventory for stateside training with ground units.

77th Reconnaissance Group — Included P-39s in its roster for mostly stateside training of ground

A group of pilots at Ephrata Army Airfield, Washington, posed for a photo while checking a map by the nose of a bare-metal P-63, circa August 1944. Front corner of main gear door extends forward to a point more pronounced than on P-39 doors. Scissors on nosewheel strut face forward on P-63, and aft on P-39s. (AFHRA)

Silver P-39N-5 (42-18818) rises from the Ephrata, Washington, runway, its electrically-driven landing gear already retracting. Nose gear brace is starting to fold at mid-point hinge. (Air Force photo)

units. (A detachment went to India between February and July 1943, but it is not known if this included any P-39s.)

81st Fighter Group — Trained with P-39s in 1942 before going to North Africa under 12th Air Force later that year to begin combat in January 1943. This unit had some P-39s overseas as late as February 1944.[5]

318th Fighter Group — Included P-39s in its training and patrols around the Hawaiian Islands from October 1942 into 1944.[6]

328th Fighter Group — Assigned to 4th Air Force and based at Hamilton Field, California between 1942 and 1944, this unit served as an air defense component and also trained replacement P-39 pilots.

332nd Fighter Group — Activated 13 October 1942, the 332nd trained with P-39s and P-40s before beginning operations in 12th Air Force in early 1944, using P-39s for convoy escort, armed reconnaissance, and harbor protection between February and April, before changing aircraft and numbered air force assignments.

338th Fighter Group — Trained replacement pilots in Florida on a variety of aircraft including P-39s circa 1942-43.

339th Fighter Group — Converting from A-24s and A-25s to P-39s in July 1943, the 339th trained and participated in stateside maneuvers with their Airacobras before moving to England to fly P-51s in 1944.

342nd Composite Group — Activated on 11 September 1942 in Iceland, this group was equipped with P-39s, P-38s, P-40s and a B-18 bomber.

347th Fighter Group — Assigned to 13th Air Force, the 347th used P-400s and P-39s at Guadalcanal in 1943; by summer 1944, the unit was equipped with P-38 Lightnings.

350th Fighter Group — Used P-39s and P-400s (plus a few P-38s) in North Africa and the Mediterranean with 12th Air Force from January 1943 to the end of July 1944, when it converted to P-47s.

354th Fighter Group — Activated on 15 November 1942, the 354th trained with P-39s and formed part of the continental United States' air defenses before moving to England and flying P-51s late in 1943.

357th Fighter Group — This fighter group, activated on the first of December 1942, used P-39s to train for combat at stations including Tonopah Army Airfield, Nevada, where future P-51 ace Charles E. "Chuck" Yeager first met up with the Airacobra early in 1943. The 357th entered combat on 11 February 1944 as an 8th Air Force Mustang group.

P-39Ds launch in 1942 on stateside maneuvers. Wing dihedral, necessary for stability, is evident on aircraft facing camera. Propeller is turning faster on flying aircraft than those still on the ground, as evidenced by "bending" illusion on airborne prop blades, induced by the camera shutter. (Bell via USAFM)

363rd Fighter Group — Trained with P-39s in California in 1943 before becoming a 9th Air Force P-51 outfit.

367th Fighter Group — Trained with P-39s in California in 1943 before becoming a 9th Air Force P-38 group in 1944.

369th Fighter Group — Trained crews and participated on a variety of stateside maneuvers with aircraft including P-39s, circa 1943-45.

404th Fighter-Bomber Group — A redesignated dive bomb group that later surfaced as a 9th Air Force P-47 fighter group, the 404th used P-39s and other aircraft in training circa 1943.

405th Fighter Group — Included P-39s in its training phase in the southeastern United States in 1943; next year became a 9th Air Force P-47 unit.

415th Bombardment Group — this dive-bomber group included some P-39s in its inventory. The unit served as a training and demonstration organization at the USAAF School of Applied Tactics, and later as a replacement training unit until its disbandment in April 1944.

432nd Reconnaissance Group — P-39s were in this group, which last-ed less than a year during 1943, during which it was assigned to the USAAF School of Applied Tactics, and later, served in a training capacity for fighter, bomber, and ground units.

478th Fighter Group — A short-lived replacement training group that only had P-39s on hand for the month of March 1944 at Redmond Army Airfield, Oregon, at the end of which the unit was disbanded.

Other USAAF organizations, not technically classified as combat units, operated P-39s and P-63s in training roles, often for the benefit of bomber gunner trainees. Peak inventory of P-39s on hand in the USAAF was 2,150 Airacobras in Feb-

While a crowd watched from the hilltop in the background, a parked P-39D-1 (41-28353) at a wartime airpower demonstration near Spokane, Washington, circa 1944, cut loose with gunfire that enveloped the landing gear in clouds of dust. P-39s were scrapped in Spokane at war's end. (Air Force photo)

ruary 1943. As American combat and training use of the P-39 dwindled, the number of P-39s in the AAF dropped to only 22 by August 1945; in the peacetime month of December 1945, only one Airacobra was carried by the Army Air Forces. P-63s in U.S. service topped out at 346 Kingcobras in May 1945.[7]

As the only USAAF combat fighter carrying a 37-MM cannon, the P-39's activities show up in minute detail in a statistical study by the Air Force of ammunition expended worldwide during the Second World War. Categorized by operational areas, USAAF P-39s expended potent 37-millimeter cannon rounds as shown in the chart below.

37MM AMMUNITION FIRED				
THEATER OF OPERATIONS	**1942**	**1943**	**1944**	**TOTAL**
MEDITERRANEAN (MTO)	—	6,000	7,000	13,000
PACIFIC OCEAN (7TH AF)	—	1,000	1,000	2,000
FAR EAST AF (5TH, 13TH AFS)	—	16,000	90,000	106,000
ALASKA	1,000	1,000	—	2,000

Smiling crewmen posed in front of a line of 71st Tactical Recon Group P-39Qs on an earthen flightline in New Guinea, circa 1944. Aircraft nearest camera retained its original yellow-over-olive serial number on the tail, with white tail paint overspray evident. Fourth P-39 in line, while a Q-model, has been fitted with the older balloon smooth-contour nose tire. Compare relative size of tire and wheel with that of third aircraft in line, which has the low-profile nose tire. (Larry Jaynes collection)

Even the omnitient statisticians of the Army Air Forces may have had some gaps in their coverage; the Alaska figures for 1942 represent March through December, and the absence of any 5th Air Force tally for 1942 seems curious. What the statistics do show is an overwhelming predominance of 37-MM expenditures by Far East Air Forces (FEAF), especially by 1944, the last year of Airacobra combat opera-

tions with the USAAF. By 1944, the tough little P-39 was in its prime as a ground attack machine in FEAF. Total overseas expenditure of 37-MM ammunition, as tallied by the AAF, amounted to 123,000 rounds.[8]

The P-39 and P-63 had limited roles in the wartime Army Air Forces. Their once-cutting-edge designs were out of date by war's end, as jet fighters and fighter-bombers took their place in the skies. But the same ability

to reach out for a new concept remained with Bell Aircraft Corporation, whose bullet-shaped orange X-1 rocket aircraft roared into world history on 14 October 1947, as former P-39 pilot Capt. Charles E. "Chuck" Yeager became the first person to fly faster than the speed of sound. Arguably, it took the fiscal stability of large production orders for P-39s and P-63s to keep the Bell company going, and to allow its designers to create the innovative, and successful, X-1.

New P-39Cs of the 39th Pursuit Squadron, 31st Pursuit Group, pass muster with pilots in line at Selfridge Field, Michigan, circa 1941. Aircraft nearest camera has bulged fairing over gun ports in top of nose; next P-39 in line has gun ports exposed. Cannons are not fitted. Compare slight backward castering appearance of P-39 nosewheel forks to straight-line side view of a P-63 nose strut. P-39 main gear doors were more nearly semi-circular in silhouette than Kingcobra main wheel doors. (USAFM)

[1] Message, Gen. MacArthur, GHQ SWPA, to CG AAF (Gen. Arnold), Subject (not delineated on document): Air combat comparisons of P-39, P-40, and Japanese "0" fighters, 14 May 1942. [2] Maurer Maurer, *Air Force Combat Units of World War II*, Office of Air Force History, Washington, DC, 1983. [3] History report, 71st Reconnaissance Group, 1 May - 31 May 1944, dated 14 July 1944 (at AFHRA). [4] Maurer Maurer, *Air Force Combat Units of World War II*, Office of Air Force History, Washington, DC, 1983. [5] Kenn C. Rust, *Twelfth Air Force Story*, Historical Aviation Album, Temple City, California, 1975. [6] Maurer Maurer, *Air Force Combat Units of World War II*, Office of Air Force History, Washington, DC, 1983. [7] *Army Air Forces Statistical Digest — World War II —* USAAF HQ, Office of Statistical Control, December 1945, and Supplement Number 1: 1945, April 1946. [8] *Army Air Forces Statistical Digest — World War II —* USAAF HQ, Office of Statistical Control, December 1945.

TUMBLING P-39s: MYTH OR REALITY

AIRACOBRA INFLIGHT EMERGENCIES

The P-39 was an unusual aircraft. Its tricycle landing gear, long drive shaft, huge cannon, diminutive dimensions and center-mounted engine were bound to raise eyebrows. When pilots encountered violent maneuvers under some circumstances, it was easy to interpret the radical movements of the aircraft as tumbling.

When the Army Air Forces monitored a P-39 in 1943 during a series of maneuvers in an effort to duplicate, or debunk, the stories of P-39s tumbling, the testers could not create a tumble.[1]

The narration to a wartime (formerly restricted) film about the phenomenon noted: "The inverted spin of a P-39 is somewhat more violent, but otherwise similar to its normal spin," adding, "…the spin is more oscillatory than the average student pilot is accustomed to."[2] This suggests a belief by the testers that some of the reports of tumbling P-39s could have been the earnest explanations of inexperienced fliers who did not fully realize what they were experiencing.

The film documented different attempts to tumble the Airacobra, during which a total of more than 1,000 spin turns were counted. "The nearest approach to tumbling was caused by pushing the stick forward sharply near stalling speed following a vertical climb. With the stick held forward, the plane begins an inverted spin, and falls in an erratic fashion — slow, then fast, and always swaying in an oscillatory manner to the left. There was a normal recovery. Repeated attempts at this same type of maneuver produced almost the same effect."[3]

One test called for the pilot to pull back on the stick in a steep climb as in the beginning of a loop, causing airspeed to bleed off. "As the plane slows down, it begins to roll and almost does an immelman, which the pilot is unable to stop, and does a portion of a turn of an inverted spin and makes a recovery." Still, the testers could find no true tumble.

"In many attempts, no maneuver could be achieved which was at all out of the ordinary," the filmed narration noted.[4]

"The rapid spins and snap rolls could be misinterpreted at first glance as an end-over-end tumbling motion. However, in no case did the airplane do one complete tumble. The test also shows that the so-called tumbling of a P-39 is really a maneuver which combines inverted snap rolls, inverted spins, normal

A liberal coating of Nevada desert dust attests to the violent energy expended as an early production P-39D (41-6746) ground to a halt at Las Vegas Army Airfield on 13 June 1944. The engine was turning when the aircraft hit ground, as all three propeller blades are crumpled back. Impact was severe enough to deform cockpit and pop out sections of Plexiglas. Nose gear, ripped from its brackets, rests out by the wing. (Nellis AFB via Marty Isham)

spins, and the usual result of too-vigorous application of forward stick pressure retained for too long a time in recovering from high stalls."

Tumble or no tumble, a 1944-dated P-39N flight manual, under the heading of spins, advised: "Deliberate spinning is not recommended. The spin is oscillatory in rate and it requires about 4,000 feet for a three-turn spin." Under the heading of stalls, the manual said: "Stalling characteristics of the airplane are very good. At minimum speeds the stall is gentle and the airplane may drop off on either wing. If the control stick is kept back and the stall is continued, and if the rudder and ailerons are used to hold the airplane level, a form of falling leaf may develop which will finally result in the nose dropping, but with no vicious tendencies. At high speeds, the stall characteristics on a turn are average, with sufficient warning being given to the pilot by a shuddering of the airplane."[5]

A slick-winged P-39Q-20 (44-3586) came to rest on collapsed landing gear at Las Vegas, Nevada, on 29 December 1944, folding its gray-silver Aeroproducts propeller. Earlier repairs to the fabric rudder rendered it without serial numbers, but digits remained on the vertical fin.

There were other Airacobra handling tips that prudent pilots heeded: "With the 175-gallon auxiliary tank installed, the minimum cruise speed is 175 mph IAS [indicated airspeed]. The minimum speed for turning near the ground with the 175-gallon auxiliary tank installed is 150 mph IAS; recommended speed fur turning near the ground with the 75-gallon belly tank installed is 130 mph IAS."[6]

When All Else Fails

If a P-39 wound up in a completely untenable situation, the pilot could opt to bail out. The pilot's manual presumed the pilot could still control the P-39 prior to the bailout, and instructed: "Trim the airplane nose heavy and turn the ignition and battery switches 'OFF.' Bank slightly toward the door that is to be the exit (right hand door is recommended, since there are no obstructions on this side). Pull up almost to a stall before bailing out. Pull the emergency release handle and push out on the door; slide off wing. (The emergency release handles, painted red, are located forward of each cabin door. The door is released when the handle is pulled back approximately 90 degrees.)"[7]

One situation that could prompt a P-39 pilot to bail out was an inextinguishable fire. The pilot's manual said to "…turn off fuel selector valve, fuel pump, battery switch and the ignition switch. Place mixture control in the 'IDLE CUT-OFF' position; close throttle. Attempt to extinguish flames by diving the airplane. If the fire is put out, make a dead stick landing rather than turning on fuel again, since the latter procedure probably would re-start the fire. If impossible to extinguish

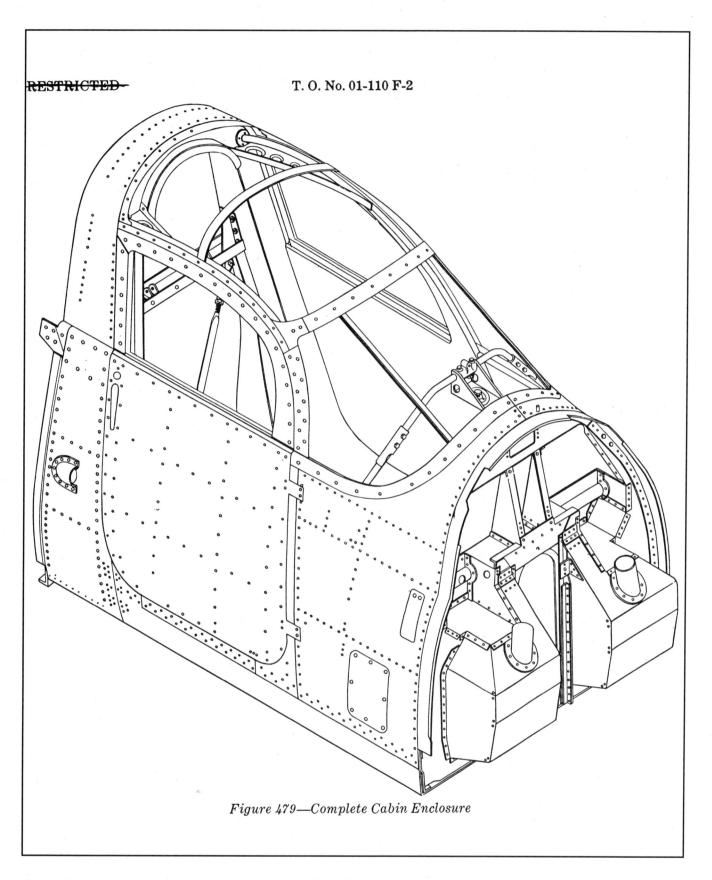

Figure 479—Complete Cabin Enclosure

From a P-39 Erection and Maintenance manual, a line drawing shows the complete Airacobra cabin assembly. Box-like structures at front of cabin are rudder pedal wells. Heavy-duty built-up aluminum rollover structure at aft end of cockpit defined curvature of cockpit at that location.

Even the stout Airacobra cabin structure could not save the life of the pilot of this overturned P-39N (42-8857) near Ephrata, Washington, on 8 May 1944. The aircraft shows evidence of ventral damage before flipping on its back, and appears to have come to rest with its gear retracted. P-39 pilots were told to keep landing gear retracted if a forced landing on soft ground was anticipated. (Air Force photo)

this design, since the tail is liable to burn away during the final stages and cause the airplane to fall out of control when the pilot is too low to bail out. A considerable amount of individual judgment is necessary in such cases."[8]

Unlike the P-51 Mustang, whose underslung engine coolant scoop beneath the aft fuselage made it so dangerous to ditch the Mustang that the pilot's manual advised against it except when all other options were exhausted, the P-39 manual had no such warnings about ditching the Airacobra. The P-39 pilot was told to "…retract the landing gear, extend flaps, drop belly tank, lock harness back, release the parachute harness, and RELEASE BOTH DOORS PRIOR TO HITTING THE WATER."[9]

the flames by diving, skidding or slipping, and if impossible to make an immediate landing, fly airplane to a safe altitude and away from populated districts and continue attempts to extinguish flames as long as practical. If still unsuccessful, abandon the airplane. It is extremely dangerous to attempt to land a badly flaming airplane of

When releasing either the belly tank or the bomb, the pilot was told: "When it is necessary to drop a belly tank or bomb in flight, pull the bomb release handle and at the same time lift the airplane gently from the falling tank or bomb by pulling back slightly on the stick. Do not pull the nose up so sharply that the tail drops enough to strike the falling object."[10]

For off-runway emergency landings, the Airacobra pilot was told to keep the landing gear retracted if the ground was rough or soft, or extend it if the surface was smooth and hard. "If in doubt," the flight manual advised, "leave the gear retracted." The use of full flaps was advised. "As the airplane nears the ground, it is advisable to lower the flaps and land with as high an angle of attack as possible (tail down)."[11]

A shrouded cockpit and investigating police and Army officers tell a grim story. The first P-39D of the second batch ordered by the Air Force (41-6722) crashed on a farm, evidently with little lateral travel after impact. The propeller buried into the cultivated earth; virtually every part of the fuselage was bent on impact; aft fuselage tore open.

[1] *P-39 Spin and Tumble Tests, August 1st to 5th, 1943*, AAF Engineering Division Technical Report WF 08-65 (motion picture). [2] *Ibid.* [3] *Ibid.* [4] *Ibid.* [5] *Pilot's Flight Operating Instructions for Army Models P-39N-0, P-39N-1 and P-39N-5 Airplanes*, Tech Order No. 01-110-FM-1, 1 July 1944, revised 30 August 1944. [6] *Ibid.* [7] *Ibid.* [8] *Ibid.* [9] *Ibid.* [10] *Ibid.* [11] *Ibid.*

PINBALL

A NEW DIMENSION IN GUNNERY TRAINING REALISM

World War Two combat quickly unmasked some erroneous notions about defensive firepower carried by bombers. While gunners and gun emplacements were vital to bomber survival, the unyielding reality of experience showed USAAF flexible gunnery training lacked authenticity. In an effort to give newly-trained gunners the best possible training, a variety of moving target ranges were devised.

And yet, no amount of simulation (ball turret gunners sometimes practiced following toy trains on serpentine tracks inside training buildings lined with turrets) could replace actual combat scenarios. A bold proposal sought to use aircraft, with toughened skins, as targets to be fired upon by new gunners using live ammunition of a special design. The realism was

The most radical gunnery training scheme to come out of the cauldron of World War Two was the Pinball armored manned target program. Heavily-plated RP-63 Kingcobras made mock fighter attacks on bombers equipped with special .30-caliber guns, manned by student gunners who fired disintegrating bullets directly at the unarmed Kingcobras. Four Pinballs in flight show two types of modified carburetor scoop. A low-profile crescent on the first aircraft could still ingest frangible bullet fragments; second RP-63 in formation has a flush carburetor inlet to avoid scooping bullet fragments. (USAFM)

compelling; the mock attackers would execute real pursuit curves and imitate Axis fighter tactics against bombers carrying student gunners over American ranges. The students would take aim and fire directly at the attackers; the frangible bullets would disintegrate upon impacting the thick skin of the special flying targets. The AAF began development of a lead-and-plastic frangible bullet in mid-1942.

It was an ideal mission for the admittedly short-legged P-63. Not

used by the USAAF as an escort fighter overseas, the Kingcobra could be used as a designated aggressor at home, where range was secondary to other considerations. But before the P-63 was selected and modified for use as a manned aerial target, the twin-engine Douglas A-20 attack bomber was favored for the role. A section of A-20 wing was clad in armor made of duralumin, and early in 1944 it survived static firing tests. Next came the plating of a complete A-20, suitably nicknamed

RP-63C-2 (43-11074) has curved louver horizontal labyrinth baffles in wing root coolant inlets, intended to deflect frangible bullets. Fragments of the disintegrating projectiles still occasionally slipped past the steel baffles to damage coolant radiators. Heavier canopy ribbing is evident; glazing was armor glass to protect pilot. Aft canopy on Pinballs was thick metal for armor protection. Stainless steel angled plates protected each exhaust stack from hits. (Gordon S. Williams via Peter M. Bowers)

Alclad Nag, for live fire and flight testing in Florida. But the big multi-engine bomber was obviously handicapped by all the added weight of the armor, and successful though the actual firing trials were, the AAF decided any production target aircraft should be more like the Messerschmitt Me-109 in traits. During this phase of the frangible bullet program, the relative availability of P-63s versus Mustangs and Thunderbolts made the Kingcobra ever more attractive.[1]

Typical base color for RP-63 Pinballs was orange (probably International Orange) to make the attackers readily visible to student gunners. Yet against a dark blue sky, orange can sometimes be less visible than white. This RP-63C-2 (43-10972) appears to be hedging its bet with white stripes over its base orange coat. (Fred Bamberger collection via Peter M. Bowers)

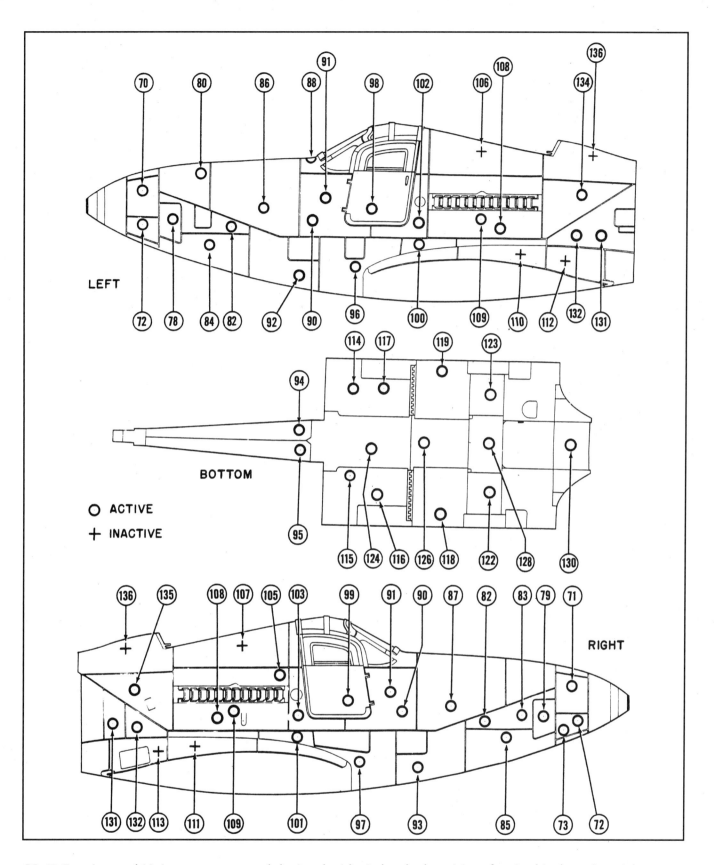

RP-63 Erection and Maintenance manual depicted with circles the locations of active hit-detecting pick-ups on forward fuselage bolt-on armor plates. Drawing also portrays smaller sized door windows, and armor glass top canopy windows which appear to have one-way curvature instead of more difficult compound curve. Exhaust stack baffle plates cover the vulnerable exhaust stacks. (Bill Miranda collection)

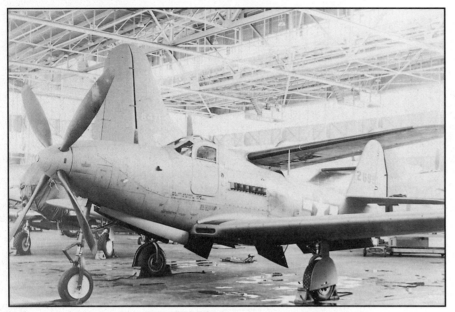

Bell took more than a passing interest in the frangible bullet program when their P-63 was chosen to be the armored target. The typical Bell enthusiasm and inventiveness were assets. As envisioned, the RP-63s in this program were armored to protect them from gunners firing during a classic pursuit curve, with plating to protect pilot and aircraft from bullets in a cone radiating 30 degrees from the RP-63s' line of flight. Gunnery students were expected to stop firing before the RP-63 made its break from the pursuit curve, but in eagerness, some students literally shot down RP-63s with a well-placed frangible bullet in a vulnerable part of the target Kingcobra.[2]

The necessary armor was up to a quarter-inch thick — too much for production P-63 drop-hammer processes, so the bolt-on skin plates for the first RP-63s were largely hand rolled and pounded with small sledge hammers. By August of 1944, the prototype RP-63 flew, followed by a production order for 95 RP-63As. The whole notion of placing sensors under the skin plates, allowing hits to be counted

and also heralded by a blinking light in the RP-63's propeller spinner, gave rise to naming one of the three prototypes Pinball, the name that stuck to the whole program.

For RP-63A-11 through RP-63C-2 variants, the hit indicator system used 109 pick-up units to electronically record hits by frangible bullets. A test of the system could be performed on the ground by striking any of the sections of armor-plated skin that contained an active pick-up sensor. According to an RP-63 erection and maintenance manual: "In addition to recording such hits the system also visually indicates hits to pilot of target airplane, and gunners who are firing at target airplane, by means of lights which flash as hits are made." The manual described the mechanics of hit sensing: "Pick-ups are of the Magnetostriction type and consist of a permanent magnet core which is wound with a stator coil... Vibration caused by impact of bullets on armor plate to which pick-up is attached, causes stress variation in the permanent magnet. These stress variations produce changes in magnetic flux causing

the lines of force to move across the coil, thereby inducing an alternating current of low voltage in the stator coil. Voltage of current generated is proportional to rate of change in stress, therefore, amplitude and frequency of vibration governs intensity of the signal generated. Voltage thus generated is applied to a mixer unit and amplifier through a shielded cable and junction box." Mechanics were cautioned not to disassemble pick-up units, because they were calibrated at the factory, and disassembly could degrade this. The complex hit sensing and recording system relied on vacuum-tube technology of the era.[3]

An AAF manual described the pick-up unit installations: "Provisions are made for attaching a pick-up unit to each section of removable armor plate and to the aft fuselage and empennage skin. Each section of removable armor plate is stamped with the part number, AAF serial number of the airplane, the heat treat stamp, and the number of the pick-up unit installed on the plate... In most cases the units are attached at right angles to the plate. Holes are drilled in the airplane skin, to provide room for the pick-up unit."[4]

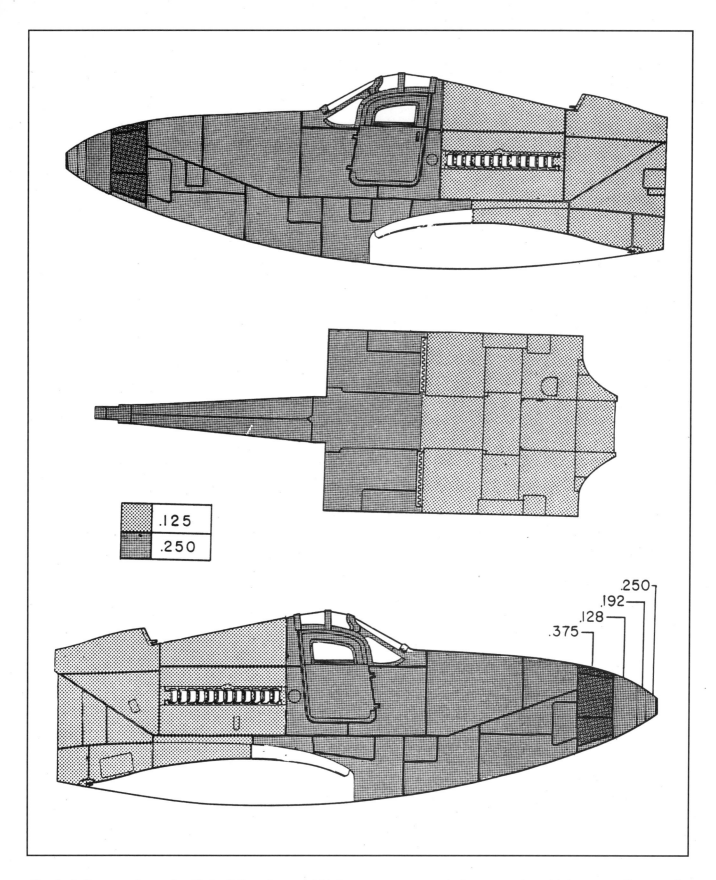

.125
.250

.250
.192
.128
.375

Shaded diagram from the Pinball Erection and Maintenance manual shows varying thicknesses of armor, in thousandths of inches, used on the forward fuselages of RP-63As through RP-63Cs, with the thickest protection toward the front. (Bill Miranda collection)

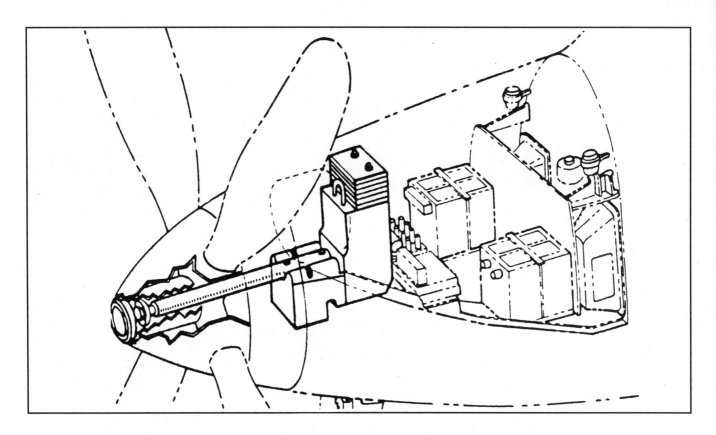

Heavy ballast block replaced weight of 37-мм cannon in the nose of RP-63, as shown in Pinball Erection and Maintenance manual. From the iron block, a tube ran forward through the propeller spinner, presenting a hit-recording flashing light to gunners, although its utility came under question. (Bill Miranda collection)

Concurrent with the creation of RP-63 Pinballs, Duke University refined .30-caliber frangible bullets to an operationally-successful degree, although some feed and trajectory problems would continue to nag the program.[5]

Part of the reason Pinball Kingcobras could withstand being shot at was the frangible bullets were small .30-caliber shapes instead of the more massive .50-caliber size in nearly universal use aboard American bombers by the time Pinball came into being. This necessitated modifying gun turrets and flexible waist mounts to take smaller .30-caliber machine guns, which had to be fine-tuned to permit rapid and continuous feeding of the unusual frangible rounds.

The original production run of RP-63As was augmented by 200 RP-63Cs, and capped off by the creation of 32 RP-63Gs. Where regular P-63 variants deleted inboard main wheel well doors, the Pinballs used doors to completely enclose and protect the tires. Early RP-63As were vulnerable to bullet ingestion in the dorsal carburetor scoop. Ideas to prevent this included facing the scoop to the rear, although RP-63As continued to be built with forward-facing carburetor inlets. The RP-63G used a flush opening in the fuselage for the carburetor.[6]

The heat-treated 24ST aluminum alloy plating that protected Pinball aircraft and pilots varied in thickness in response to the nature of impacts likely to be received on various parts of the structure. Plating thicknesses were revised on G-models, probably in response to

service use with older Pinballs. The cockpit glazing, including windscreen, doors, and overhead windows, was armor glass in Pinballs, with thicker webbing between panels than on unarmored P-63s. Rear canopy glazing was replaced by aluminum armor plate on Pinball aircraft. P-63As and Cs used built-up propeller spinners of differing laminations and thicknesses for additional protection. To stop the entry of frangible bullets into the cockpit around the two swinging doors, the RP-63 Erection and Maintenance manual noted: "Strips of steel secured on the inside of the cabin, at the forward edge of the doors, prevent the entrance of frangible bullets through the area around that part of the door and the hinges. A section of alclad installed on the outside rear edge of the door, overlaps the bottom

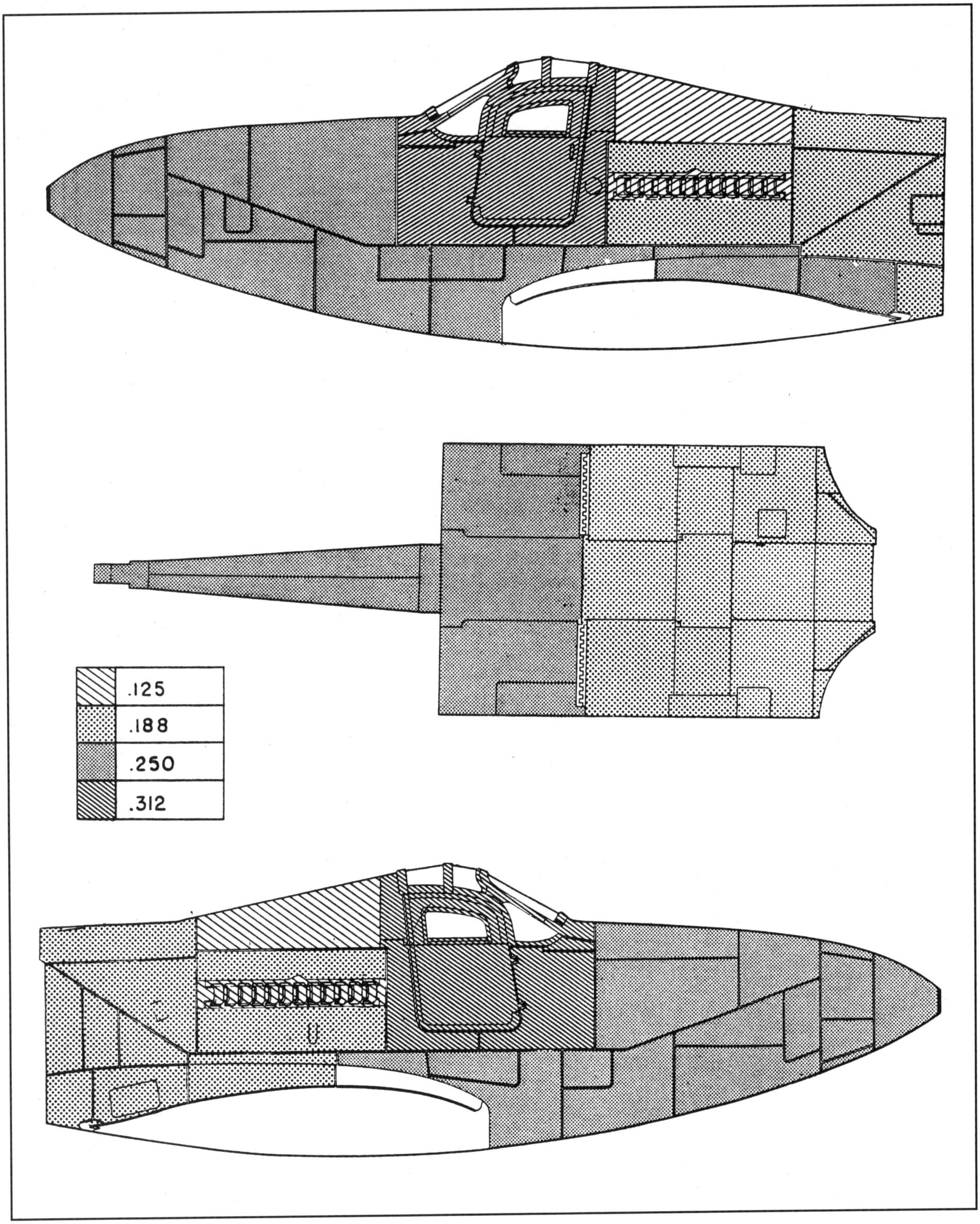
.125
.188
.250
.312

RP-63Gs, last of the Pinball line, beefed up cockpit armor plating to .312-inch thickness, while simplifying prop spinner at constant thickness. Flush carburetor inlet is depicted in this drawing from a Pinball manual. (Bill Miranda collection)

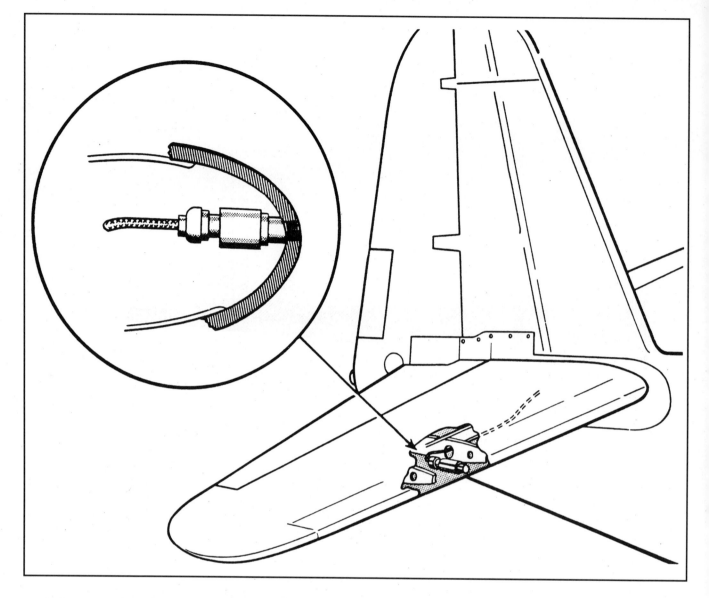

Pinball tech order drawing shows details of RP-63 hit sensor mounted in leading edge of horizontal stabilizer. Pick-ups were numbered and factory-sealed after calibration. They could be tested on the ground by striking the aircraft in the vicinity of a pick-up. Theoretically, any strike on a plate backed by a pick-up would record on a hit counter, and light up the Pinball hit registering light (or multiple lights on RP-63Gs), but accuracy of hit recording came under question. (Bill Miranda collection)

and rear openings to complete the protection around the doors. A section of steel secured to the lower edge of each door glass provides further protection against bullets striking the area."[7]

The forward fuselage and wings of RP-63s were protected by armor plate attached by screws or ubiquitous aircraft Dzus fasteners. Armor panels that screwed onto the struc-ture over existing skin relied on floating nut plates mounted to reinforcements in the original skin; the floating nut plates made installation and alignment of the armor plating easier. Some access doors were replaced with Dzus-fastened armor panels. The empennage and aft fuselage of RP-63s were built with flush-riveted heavy 24ST alclad skin .091-inches thick, with heavier plating screwed to the leading edges of the vertical fin and horizontal stabilizer.[8]

Exhaust stubs were protected by angled steel shrouds attached with Dzus fasteners. Labyrinth steel baffles in the cooling inlets in the wings was supposed to baffle frangible bullet fragments from damaging the delicate cooling system [although this was a source of problems for RP-63 operations]. The

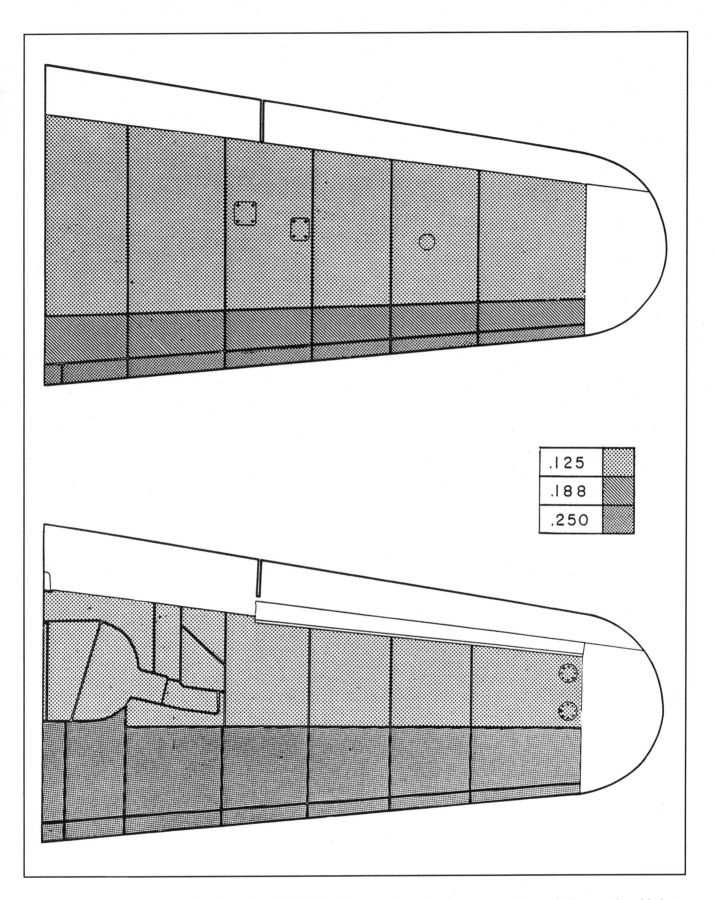

Frontal .250-inch protection for RP-63A and RP-63C wings was heavier than aft portions which were less likely to receive damage. (Bill Miranda collection)

Hordes of orange Pinball Kingcobras swarmed the ramp at Laredo Army Airfield, Texas, in 1945. Blotches on national insignia of aircraft nearest camera might include frangible bullet impacts on the thick-skinned aft fuselage. (AFHRA)

RP-63 manual said horizontal baffles in the entrance of the inlet were "curved so that bullets cannot pass beyond them." Evidently, fragments nonetheless managed to rattle past the baffles on occasion.[9]

Movable control surfaces were also armor skinned for protection. The array of armor plate on RP-63As and RP-63Cs provided protection within 30 degrees of head-on for the Pinball; RP-63G-1 versions were additionally protected from broadside hits. And in case an ambitious student gunner continued firing at a Pinball flying away fromt the gunner, aluminum armor .250-inches thick was installed in the turnover beam behind the pilot's head, augmenting the thick skin that replaced the aft cabin windows.[10]

The unarmed RP-63s were fitted with an N-3C gunsight to give the Pinball pilot a realistic view of his quarry when executing fighter tactics. The absence of a 37-MM cannon and two .50-caliber machine guns in the nose of RP-63s demanded substitution of a cast iron ballast

block between the longitudinal beams in the nose, behind the reduction gearbox. On RP-63A-11 through RP-63C-2 versions, the ballast block weighed about 430 pounds; when RP-63G-1s were fitted with radio equipment in the forward fuselage compartment, the ballast block was reduced to about 362 pounds for these Pinballs.[11]

By the end of April 1945, student gunners at Las Vegas Army Airfield in the starkly beautiful Nevada desert were shooting frangible bullets at Pinball RP-63s, according to a contemporary history from Las Vegas AAF, "but the results were not very satisfactory. About 5 percent hits were recorded. However, it was undetermined whether the error was in the number of hits or whether the hit counters used were not operating sufficiently to record all of the hits made."[12]

Most vexing to the Pinball program was the incidence of frangible bullet fragments finding their way into the cooling system of the RP-63 by way of the wing leading edge-

mounted inlets. Louvers were put in front of the openings as an aid.[13]

But by July of 1945, the research division of the USAAF Central School for Flexible Gunnery at Laredo Army Airfield, Texas, noted in its monthly project status report: "All RP-63s have been grounded throughout the Training Command and Training Air Forces. However, the Research Division has received special permission to use 10 of these aircraft solely for experimental purposes. The grounding of these aircraft is the result of the effects of small fragments of the frangible projectile lodging in the air coolers of the RP-63s."[14]

Even as the RP-63s were grounded, work continued to upgrade the bombers used in training Pinball gunners. B-29s, with central fire control and remotely-sighted turrets, were being phased in to the Pinball program instead of the B-17s and B-24s originally intended. For July 1945, the USAAF Central School for Flexible Gunnery reported: "The greatest portion of the work being accomplished by the Frangible Bullet Section during [this month] is directly concerned with the modification of B-29 equipment." The report continued: "All positions except the upper forward have been installed and tested on the B-29. Considerable difficulty has been encountered in the charger mount." Substitution of chrome moly steel for cold-rolled steel in some of the charger parts

RP-63 aft fuselages were armored chiefly by making them with thicker integral skins, although bolt-on leading edges were added for still greater protection. RP-63G addressed strike problems with tail leading edges of .375 thousandths of an inch in thickness. (Bill Miranda collection)

appeared to correct the problem. By that time, not only Laredo had a frangible-firing B-29; Las Vegas, Harlingen, and Second Air Force each possessed a B-29 so modified.[15] But the war was nearly over; although Strategic Air Command showed interest in RP-63 training in the immediate postwar era, the window of opportunity for Pinball Kingcobras was closing as the jet age dawned with new bombers, new capabilities, and new potential adversaries. Pinball remains as one of the most unorthodox, and potentially realistic, gunnery training plans ever devised. If its execution was beset by problems, its concept smacked of Yankee ingenuity.

[1] Ivan Hickman, *Operation Pinball — The USAAF's Secret Aerial Gunnery Program in WWII*, Motorbooks, Osceola, Wisconsin, 1990. [2] *Ibid.* [3] Excerpt from RP-63 Erection and Maintenance manual AN 01-110FP-2A. [4] *Ibid.* [5] Ivan Hickman, *Operation Pinball — The USAAF's Secret Aerial Gunnery Program in WWII*, Motorbooks, Osceola, Wisconsin, 1990. [6] Birch Matthews, *Cobra! Bell Aircraft Corporation — 1934-1946*, Schiffer, Atglen, Pennsylvania 1996. [7] Excerpt from RP-63 Erection and Maintenance manual AN 01-110FP-2A. [8] *Ibid.* [9] *Ibid.* [10] *Ibid.* [11] *Ibid.* [12] *History of 3021st AAF Base Unit (Flexible Gunnery School), Las Vegas, Nevada; 3022d AAF Base Unit (Flexible Gunnery School), Indian Springs, Nevada, and Las Vegas Army Air Field, Las Vegas, Nevada*, March-April 1945 (original filed at USAF Historical Research Agency, Maxwell AFB, Alabama). [13] Birch Matthews, *Cobra! Bell Aircraft Corporation — 1934-1946*, Schiffer, Atglen, Pennsylvania 1996. [14] *Monthly Project Status Report*, Research Division #8, Liaison Division #11, for the month of July 1945, by Research Division, AAF Central School for Flexible Gunnery, Laredo AAF, Laredo, Texas. [15] *Ibid.*

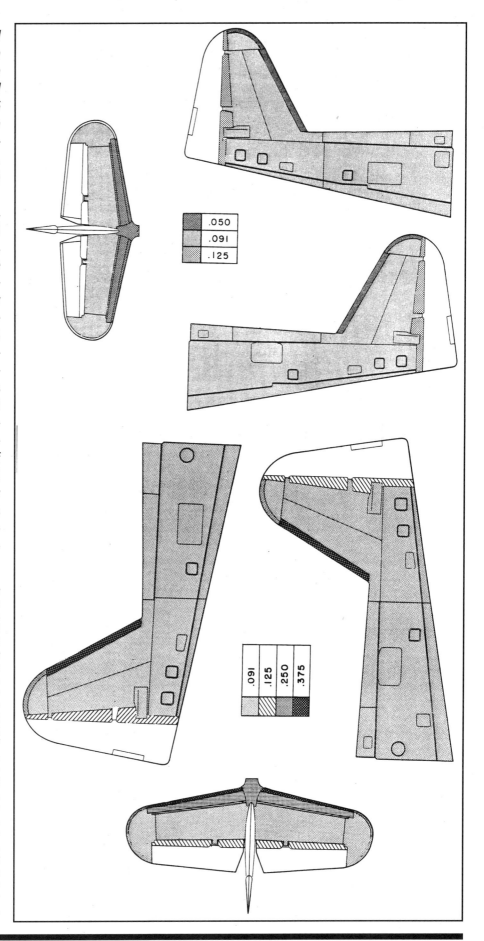

CIVILIAN 8 COBRAS

In the greatest irony of its eventful lifespan, the Bell P-39 Airacobra, sometimes vilified in combat for slow speeds, became a world-beater in post-World War Two air racing. P-39s and P-63s entered the civilian market in adequate numbers to help flesh out race rosters. Though attrition has claimed many of these 'Cobras, some survive as museum pieces or refurbished warbirds.

In the 1970s, the biggest boost to the known population of P-39s came when warbird collector David Tallichet sponsored the retrieval of as many as 13 abandoned Airacobra airframes from New Guinea. In varying states of completeness, the Tallichet cache of P-39s has largely been dispersed around the United States, with several aircraft under restoration.

Other 'Cobra survivors remain more enigmatic, like the Pinball P-63 once on display at the University of Utah campus in Salt Lake City, and now seemingly lost to memory. Coincidentally, according to aircraft researcher Milo Peltzer, in the early 1960s, about the time the Salt Lake City P-63 dropped from sight, a Pinball Kingcobra was put on display in Fresno, California. This Fresno airport Pinball was later removed, and may be reincarnated as a display elsewhere. It remains to be deciphered if the Salt Lake and Fresno Kingcobra displays represent the same airframe. The roster of surviving P-39s and P-63s is fluid as airplanes change owners, new restorations debut, and, sometimes, existing aircraft crash.

P-39s and P-63s known to have

The Confederate Air Force's P-39Q, ex-Mr. Mennen, (civil registration N40A), cruised over the south Texas farmscape in October 1976, with Ed Messick at the controls during the legendary annual warbird extravaganza at Harlingen. Painted like a south Pacific USAAF P-400, N40A was campaigned for awhile by the CAF before going to the Kalamazoo Air Museum in Michigan. Visible in the flat-fronted P-63 windscreen frame installed during one of this Airacobra's rebuilds. (Photo by Frederick A. Johnsen)

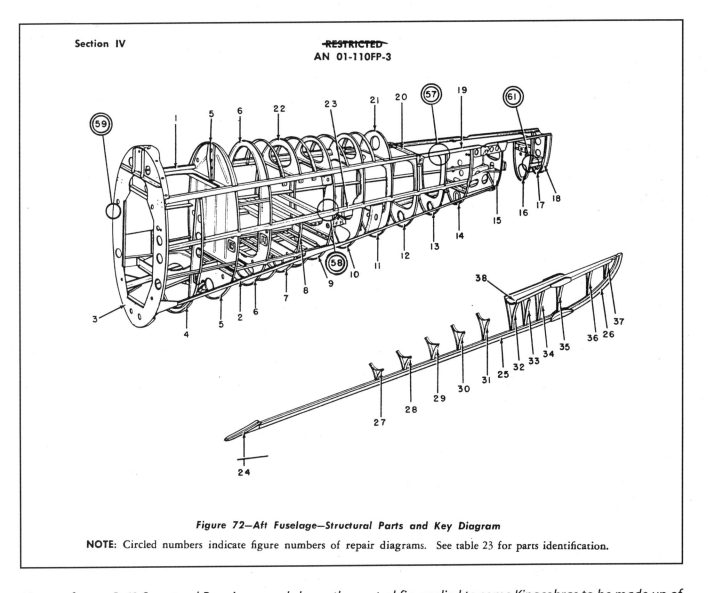

Figure 72—Aft Fuselage—Structural Parts and Key Diagram

NOTE: Circled numbers indicate figure numbers of repair diagrams. See table 23 for parts identification.

Line art from a P-63 Structural Repair manual shows the ventral fin applied to some Kingcobras to be made up of saddle-shaped ribs conforming to the existing aft fuselage structure. A keel forms the bottom; aluminum skin was applied over the structure.

crossed over into civilian registration or museums include:

P-39Q (42-20733), U.S. civil registration number NX92847, was the red-orange Cobra I racing mount of popular Bell test pilot Jack Woolams. One of a pair of Airacobras bought by Bell Aircraft as surplus, just so their three-blade propellers could be used on the Navy's L-39 program, this P-39Q was modified and groomed for air racing in 1946. Uprated with a V-1710-135 engine (still using a single-stage supercharger since the small P-39 did not accommodate the two-stage supercharger), this P-39 had other lightening and clean-up touches applied, plus a four-blade paddle propeller from a P-63E. Fuel capacity was doubled, and a water injection system added. For the 1946 Thompson trophy race, Woolams qualified the Cobra I at a respectable 392.73 miles an hour. Before the actual race, on a test hop, the highly-experienced Woolams crashed in Cobra I into Lake Ontario. Speculation about the cause centered around the possibility the windscreen somehow failed due to high loads imposed on the racer in flight, or that the aft fuselage had suffered a structural failure.

P-39Q (42-20869), U.S. civil registration NX92848, was stablemate to Jack Woolams' ill-fated racer, and carried the nickname Cobra II, and a bright yellow and black paint scheme for the 1946 Thompson trophy race. Legendary test pilot Alvin M. "Tex" Johnston flew this modified P-39 to victory in the

Eight of the P-39s retrieved from New Guinea in the 1970s by Dave Tallichet rested at the Barstow-Daggett, California, airport in January 1978, before being relocated to Chino, California. Many of these Airacobras have since been dispatched to other parts of the U.S. where they are undergoing restoration. Three of their number have been placed on static display in upstate New York, Virginia, and at Ed Maloney's Planes of Fame museum in Chino. (Photo by Frederick A. Johnsen)

1946 Thompson race, qualifying as the fastest racer that year at a remarkable 409.1 miles an hour, and winning the multi-lap race at an average speed of nearly 374 miles an hour. Among the modifications applied to the Bell-modified Cobras was a faster gear-retraction motor that helped clean up Johnston's fighter quickly as it leaped into the sky at the start of the race.

With other owners and pilots, N92848 entered races in subsequent years, before becoming part of the museum stable of Ed Maloney's museum at Ontario, California. In the late 1960s, Mike Carroll bought the former Cobra II and began a substantial modification program to clip the wings and otherwise ready it for another career in air racing. In the offing was a plan to replicate this famous racer's markings pattern, this time in white with gold trim, and the name Cobra III.[1] On a test hop, the dicey racer went out of control, and struck Carroll as he bailed out, killing him.

P-39Q (44-3908), U.S. civil registration number N40A, earlier registered NX4829N, was a former two-seat conversion reverted to single seat configuration. Its civilian owners included cross-country and pylon racer E.D. Weiner and later aerobatic pilot and hydroplane racer Mira Slovak. This P-39's former two-seat status was evident after it was reverted, since it retained the dorsal and ventral fins, and exhibited a slightly altered contour of the upper nose panel. When first reverted to single-seat, a nonstandard one-piece Plexiglas windscreen met the overhead canopy at a different place than did a factory-built single seat Airacobra windscreen and canopy combination. After Mira Slovak acquired N40A and began modifying it for racing, a flat P-63 windscreen assembly was installed.

Bell (and later Boeing) pilot A.M. "Tex" Johnston strapped on his helmet inside the bright yellow and black Cobra II racer in which he won the 1946 Thompson Trophy race at 373.9 miles an hour after qualifying at a remarkable 409 miles an hour. Nonstandard extended carburetor inlet is visible at far left behind canopy. Auxiliary oil cooler duct, incorporating P-40 engine radiator, can be seen on centerline. (Bell photo)

Slovak hoped to race N40A, nick-named *Mr. Mennen* for its sponsor, at the 1972 Reno air races, but arrived too late to qualify. Flown in some demonstrations by Slovak, the sleek green and white P-39Q subsequently was operated by Confederate Air Force supporter Ed Messick, receiving a P-400-style camouflage scheme at this time, and deleting the extra dorsal and ventral fins. Flown for several Confederate Air Force events in the late 1970s, by the early 1980s this P-39 was acquired for the Kalamazoo Air Museum in Michigan, still in its P-400 paint scheme, and still using a flat P-63 windscreen.

P-39Q (42-19597), U.S. Civil registration N6968, found its way from a derelict hulk in New Mexico to the Confederate Air Force collection by the 1970s.[2] Flown for many years in a Soviet-style paint scheme with red stars, this Q-model was exhibited at a USAF 50th anniversary air show in Las Vegas, Nevada, in USAAF stars in April 1997.

A P-39Q-15 (44-2433), U.S. registration NX57591, raced a few times in the postwar 1940s, nicknamed JUBA and later Galloping Gertie. This Airacobra later was displayed by the Experimental Aircraft Association in Wisconsin before going to the National Air and Space Museum collection.

P-39s on display in the United States include several static aircraft built up from airframes retrieved in New Guinea. One such is at the

Station diagram from a P-63A and C-series Structural Repair manual shows relationship of cockpit to wing on the Kingcobra. The ventral fin extends aft under the rudder. (Bill Miranda collection)

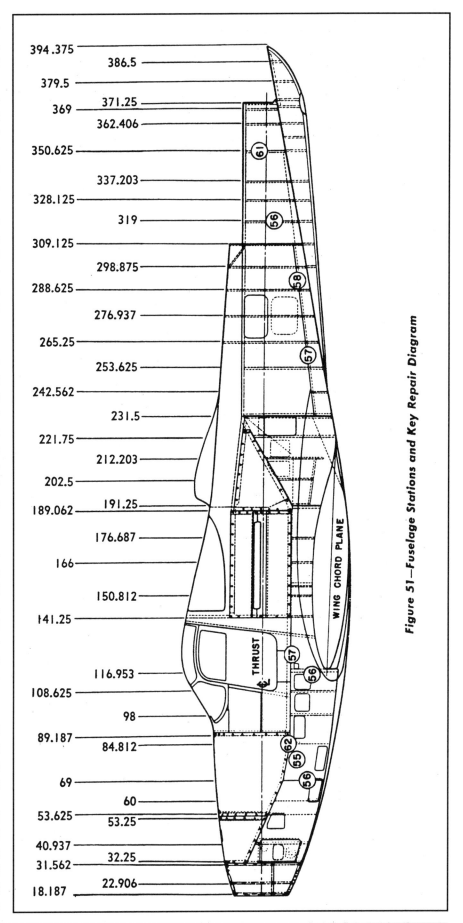

Figure 51—Fuselage Stations and Key Repair Diagram

Jack Woolams, characterized as likable and a sometime-prankster, was photographed in Cobra I, team mate to Tex Johnston's racing Airacobra, in 1946. Even the skillful Woolams could not overcome an as-yet undiscovered cause of the crash of Cobra I that cost his life before the Thompson race that year. (Bell photo)

Planes of Fame Museum in Chino, California, where it was joined in 1997 by wreckage from Soviet P-39 crashes. Another is displayed in Buffalo, New York, and a third of the New Guinea recoverees had been mounted at George Air Force Base in Victorville, California, before its transfer to a museum in Langley, Virginia. The U.S. Air Force Museum in Dayton, Ohio, displays a P-39Q (44-3887), sans wing guns.

Other Airacobras reside in Australia, New Guinea, and Guadalcanal, veterans of wartime service in the region. One example is reported in Finland.[3]

Popular on the racing and air show scene in the 1970s was a bright red P-63C (44-4393), civil registration NL62822. Ultimately this Kingcobra became part of the periodic migration of warbirds across the Atlantic Ocean to new owners; it subsequently crashed.

Photographed at the 1971 national Championship Air Races at Reno, Nevada, this innovative cut-down P-63C-5, N9009, was raced by Larry Havens. It placed fourth in the Silver race. Carburetor air was ducted through the righthand wing leading edge. If NACA tests had shown the value of lowering the XP-39's original canopy height, this P-63 took that line of thinking to its ultimate expression. This aircraft subsequently crashed in the ocean near Long Beach, California, on a test flight in 1972; Havens escaped. (Photo by Frederick A. Johnsen)

P-63E-1, serial 43-11727, civil registration N9003R, former Honduran Air Force, sold to Bob Bean Aircraft, Hawthorne, California, for $7,500 in 1960.[4] It later could be seen at the Pima Air Museum in Tucson, Arizona.

A P-63E (43-11731) returned from Honduras by Bob Bean, N9004R taxied as it was photographed in the early 1960s. This Kingcobra subsequently was destroyed by fire in 1964. (Photo by Ken Shake)

Before moving to its present site, the U.S. Air Force Museum at Wright-Patterson Air Force Base, Ohio, displayed one of the former two-seat P-63Es outdoors. When the photo was taken, the aircraft had been fitted with a patch over the rear cockpit, but no carburetor scoop protruded above the dorsal contour. The distinctive baffle atop the exhaust stacks remained in place. (E.M. Sommerich via Peter M. Bowers)

In the 1960s an RP-63 was displayed at the Fresno, California, airport. Later removed, it may survive in other Kingcobra restorations. (Photo by Frederick A. Johnsen)

P-63E-1, 43-11731, N9004R, sold to Bob Bean Aircraft, Hawthorne, California, circa 1960, was another Honduran refugee. In 1964 it was destroyed by fire in Texas.

The Air Force Museum has a P-63E; a Pinball (RP-63G 45-57295) was placed on display at Lackland Air Force base, San Antonio, Texas. Other P-63s are under restoration in the U.S. and overseas; a tall-tail P-63F was flown by the Confederate Air Force as of this writing.

One of the P-63Es (43-11734) modified by Bell with an aft observer's cockpit, this example uses a centerline ferry tank to improve time aloft. Photos of the two-seat Kingcobras show what appears to be a baffle or deflector running along the tops of the exhaust stubs, possibly to ensure exhaust did not reach the aft cockpit. Sources differ on the military serial of this

example; if it is 43-11728, then this would be the same two-seater subsequently reverted to single-seat status and put in the U.S. Air Force Museum in Ohio. (E.M. Sommerich via Peter M. Bowers)

[1] Letter, Birch Matthews to the author, 17 January 1998. [2] Rick Mitchell, *Airacobra Advantage: The Flying Cannon*, Pictorial Histories Publishing, Missoula, Montana, 1992. [3] John Chapman and Geoff Goodall, *Warbirds Worldwide Directory*, Warbirds Worldwide Ltd., Mansfield, England, 1989. [4] Bill of Sale, Honduran Air Force, to Bob Bean Aircraft, 2 February 1960; and Certificate, General Office of Civil Aviation, Honduras, with U.S. civil registration margin notes. (Records from the Malcolm Gougon collection in the library of the Flight Test Historical Museum, Edwards Air Force Base, California.)

'COBRA CHARACTERISTICS

The USAAF made a series of charts describing attributes of various P-39 and P-63 versions, based on technical orders and performance estimates. Extracted data provides an overview of major Airacobra and Kingcobra characteristics:

MODEL	DIMENSIONS	GUNS	ROUNDS/GUN	BOMBS	WEIGHT (Lbs.)	HIGH SPEED*	RANGE†
P-39D-BE	Span 34'0" Length 30'2" Height 11'10" Tread 11'4" Wing area 213 sq.ft.	4/.30-cal. 2/.50-cal. 1/37-mm.	1,000 max; 300 200 30	1/100-500lb.	6300 basic 7650 combat	324mph/25,000ft. 348mph/20,000ft. 360mph/15,000ft. 355mph/10,000ft. 335mph/5,000ft.	8850/0/295/1100 8800/0/276/1050 8150/0/195/800 7650/0/120/600 8150/500/120/450
P-39D-1BE	As above	4/.30-cal. 2/.50-cal. 1/20-mm.	1,000 max; 300 200 60	As above	As above	As above	As above
P-39D-2BE	As above	As above	As above	As above	As above	As above	As above
P-39F-BE‡	As above	4/.30-cal. 2/.50-cal. 1/37-mm.	1,000 max; 300 200 30	As above	As above	As above	As above
P-39K-1BE	As above	As above	As above	As above	As above	As above	As above
P-39L-1BE	As above	As above	As above	As above	6500 basic 7900 combat	323mph/25,000ft. 347mph/20,000ft. 360mph/15,000ft. 354mph/10,000ft. 335mph/5,000ft.	9100/0/295/1075 8400/0/195/750 7900/0/120/550 8400/500/120/400
P-39M-1BE	As above	As above	As above	As above	As above	357mph/25,000ft. 365mph/20,000ft. 370mph/15,000ft. 350mph/10,000ft. 330mph/5,000ft.	As above

'Cobra Characteristics

MODEL	DIMENSIONS	GUNS	ROUNDS/GUN	BOMBS	WEIGHT (Lbs.)	HIGH SPEED*	RANGE†
P-39N Blocks 0-5	Span 34'0" Length 30'2" Height 12'5" Tread 11'4" Wing area 213 sq.ft	As above	As above	As above	6400 basic 7600 combat	368mph/25,000ft. 375mph/20,000ft. 376mph/15,000ft. 357mph/10,000ft. 330mph/5,000ft.	8750/0/262/975 8600/0/243/900 8050/0/162/625 7550/0/87/350 8050/500/87/275
P-39Q-1BE	As above	2/.50-cal./W§ 2/.50-cal./N** 1/37-mm.	300 200 30	As above	As above	As above	As above
P-39Q-5BE	As above	As above	As above	As above	As above	As above	8900/0/285/1075 8800/0/266/1000 8200/0/185/725 7700/0/110/525 8200/500/110/375
P-39Q Blocks 10-15	As above	As above	As above	As above	As above	As above	8950/0/295/1100 8850/0/276/1050 8250/0/195/750 7750/0/120/575 8250/500/120/425
P-39Q Blocks 20-30	As above††	As above‡‡	As above	As above	As above	As above	As above
P-63A Blocks 1-7	Span 38'4" Length 32'8" Height 12'3" Tread 14'7"	2/.50-cal./W 2/.50-cal./N 1/37-mm.	250 200 30	As above (Blocks 6 & 7 also had two underwing shackles)	6925 basic 8350 combat	392mph/30,000ft. 401mph/25,000ft. 388mph/20,000ft. 372mph/15,000ft.	10500/0/451/2200 9500/0/301/1800 8850/0/201/1150 8350/0/126/740

MODEL	DIMENSIONS	GUNS	ROUNDS/GUN	BOMBS	WEIGHT (Lbs.)	HIGH SPEED*	RANGE†
	Wing area 248 sq.ft.					355mph/10,000ft. 336mph/5,000ft.	8850/500/126/650
P-63A Blocks 8-10	As above	As above§§	250 200 30(M4) 58(M10)	3/100-500lb.	As above	402mph/30,000ft. 410mph/25,000ft. 398mph/20,000ft. 380mph/15,000ft. 362mph/10,000ft. 341mph/5,000ft.	As above
P-63C-1BE	Span 384" Length 32'8" Height 12'3" Tread 14'3" Wing area 248 sq.ft.	As above with M10 cannon	As above	As above	7425 basic 8800 combat	As above	9800/0/278/1120 9300/0/203/875 8800/0/128/560 9300/500/128/475
P-63E-1BE	Span 39'2" Length 32'8" Height 12'9" Tread 15'1" Wing area 255 sq.ft.	As above (plus 3-tube underwing rocket launchers)	As above	As above	7300 basic 8900 combat	(Data not provided)	10100/0/276/1250 9500/0/201/1000 8900/0/126/675 9400/500/126/575

*Military power at normal combat weight. †Expressed as takeoff weight/bomb load/fuel gallons/longest range in miles at 10,000 ft. ‡The AAF chart does not reference the small batch of only 25 P-39Js made from the order of F-models. WS=Wing guns N**=Nose guns ††Some aircraft in these blocks had 4-blade propellers; other propeller specifications listed by the USAAF included: P-39Q-20, -21, and -25, 3-blade, 117" diameter; P-39Q-30, 3-blade, 11'0" diameter. ‡‡Some late P-39Qs deleted wing guns. §§Beginning with P-63A-9, the M10 37-mm cannon replaced the M4 variant.

'COBRA ENGINES B & PROPELLERS

New models of the P-39 and P-63 took advantage of evolving variants of the Allison V-1710 liquid-cooled V-12 engine. Additionally, Curtiss Electric and Aero Products propellers were used, with some changes, in the run of Airacobras and Kingcobras. As logged in the USAAF Tactical Planning Characteristics and Performance Chart, these engine/propeller combinations were:

MODEL	ENGINE	PROPELLER	HORSEPOWER
P-39D-BE	V-1710-35	Curtiss, 3-blade, 10'5" dia., Constant-speed electric	1150 takeoff/sea level 1150 mil. power/12000 ft. 1000 continuous/10800 ft.
P-39D-1BE	As above	As above	As above
P-39D-2BE	V-1710-63	As above	1325 takeoff/sea level 1150 mil. power/12000 ft. 1000 continuous/10800 ft.
P-39F-BE	V-1.710-35	Aero Products, 3-blade, 10'5" dia., Constant-speed hydraulic	1150 takeoff/sea level 1150 mil. power/12000 ft. 1000 continuous/10800 ft.
P-39K-1BE	V-1710-63	As above	1325 takeoff/sea level 1150 mil. power/12000 ft. 1000 continuous/10800 ft.
P-39L-1BE	As above	Curtiss, 3-blade, 10'5" dia., Constant-speed electric	As above
P-39M-1BE	V-1710-83	As above	1200 takeoff/sea level 1125 mil. power/15500 ft. 1000 continuous/14000 ft.
P-39N Blocks 0-5	V-1710-85	Aero Products, 3-blade, 11'7" dia., Constant-speed hydraulic	As above
P-39Q Blocks 1-15	As above	As above	As above
P-39Q Blocks 20-30	As above	Aero Products, 4-blade*, 11' 7" dia., Constant-speed hydraulic	As above
P-63A Blocks 1-7	V-1710-93†	Aero Products, 4-blade, 11'7" dia., Constant-speed hydraulic	1325 takeoff/sea level 1150 mil. power/24200 ft. 1000 continuous/20000 ft.
P-63A Blocks 8-10	As above	Aero Products, 4-blade, 11'0" dia., Constant-speed hydraulic	As above
P-63C-1BE	V-1710-117	As above	1325 takeoff/sea level 1100 mil. power/27000 ft. 1000 continuous/23000 ft.
P-63E-1BE	V-1710-109	Aero Products, 4-blade, 11'6" dia., Constant-speed hydraulic	1425 takeoff/sea level 1100 mil. power/28000 ft. 1050 continuous/sea level 950 continuous/24000 ft.

* A note on the USAAF Tactical Planning Characteristics and Performance Chart for 23 Feb 45 says: "Preliminary tests of P-39Q-21 and -25 show that 4-bladed propeller materially effects (sic) directional stability, but not performance." Some aircraft in these blocks had 4-blade propellers; other propeller specifications listed by the USAAF included: P-39Q-20, -21, and -25, 3-blade, 11'7" diameter; P-39Q-30, 3-blade, 11'0" diameter. † P-63s used two-stage superchargers, for markedly better performance.

SIGNIFICANT DATES

7 OCTOBER 1937
USAAC contract awarded for construction of XP-39 by Bell Aircraft Corp.

6 APRIL 1939
First flight of XP-39, at Wright Field, Ohio, where it had been shipped by rail.

19 APRIL 1940
Letter from British and French Purchasing Commissions proposed to order 200 Airacobras for France; agreement was reached with Bell, although fall of France caused this production quantity to be shifted to Great Britain.

13 MAY 1940
First flight of prototype XFL-1 Airabonita navalized version of Airacobra (BuAer No. 1588).

17 JUNE 1940
French government transferred its interest in 200-airplane Airacobra order to the British, under the shadow of imminent takeover of France by Germany.

13 SEPTEMBER 1940
First flight of a YP-39 (40-027).

JANUARY 1941
First flight of P-39C occurred this month.

27 JUNE 1941
Order placed for two XP-63 prototypes.

JULY 1941
Crated RAF Airacobra Is began arriving in UK.

26 FEBRUARY 1942
First flight of first prototype XP-39E.

MARCH 1942
Spin crash of first prototype XP-39E.

APRIL 1942
First of 15 P-39s used in service by Royal Australian Air Force delivered.

14 AUGUST 1942
First USAAF aerial victory in the European Theater of Operations (ETO) was shared by a P-39D pilot, 2 Lt. Joseph D. R. Shaffer, of the 33rd Fighter Squaqdron in Iceland, when he and a P-38 Lightning pilot from another squadron downed a Focke-Wulf FW-200 four-engine patrol bomber off the coast of Iceland. Two months later, a pair of 33rd Fighter Squadron P-39Ds logged a 55-minute running battle with a FW-200 in and out of clouds before the large Focke-Wulf headed into a cloud bank, and to presumed safety.

17 SEPTEMBER 1942
Order given to change future wing gun installations on P-39s to be two .50-caliber machine guns instead of four .30-caliber guns; this was instated on the P-39Q which first was produced in mid-1943.

7 DECEMBER 1942
First flight of XP-63 Kingcobra.

26 APRIL 1943
First flight of XP-63A.

AUGUST 1944
Last Airacobra (a P-39Q-30) delivered.

21 MARCH 1945
A P-63 from Walla Walla, Washington, intercepted a Japanese balloon bomb near Redmond, chasing it in a cross-country that necessitated two refueling stops for the Kingcobra before the fighter shot the balloon out of the sky near Reno, Nevada.

AUGUST 1946
Bell test pilot Alvin "Tex" Johnston qualified his modified P-39Q, Cobra II, for the Thompson Trophy race at 409 miles an hour and won the race with an average speed of nearly 374 miles an hour.

1951
French P-63s in combat in Indochina replaced with other fighter types.

1951
Last P-39s in Italian military service were retired; a few training and test Airacobras in French service lasted about as long.